Twayne's English Authors Series

EDITOR OF THIS VOLUME

Herbert Sussman
Northeastern University

R. D. Blackmore

TEAS 265

R. D. Blackmore

R. D. BLACKMORE

By MAX KEITH SUTTON

University of Kansas

TWAYNE PUBLISHERS
A DIVISION OF G. K. HALL & CO., BOSTON

(Street)
PR4134
.S9

Frontispiece photograph by Frederick Jenkins courtesy of the
Devon Record Office, Exeter.

Library of Congress Cataloging in Publication Data

Sutton, Max Keith.
R. D. Blackmore.

(Twayne's English authors series ; TEAS 265)
Bibliography: p. 149 - 52
Includes index.
1.   Blackmore, Richard Doddridge, 1825 - 1900—
Criticism and interpretation.
PR4134.S9   823'.8   78-31885
ISBN 0-8057-6756-8

To my father and the memory of my mother
and to the community of Cheriton Fitzpaine

Contents

About the Author

Max Keith Sutton received his B.A. from the University of Arkansas and his M.A. and Ph.D. from Duke University. His publications include articles on Browning, Hopkins, Blackmore, and Victorian humor and satire, and a book on W. S. Gilbert for the Twayne English Authors Series. His current research is on the image of rural community in nineteenth-century British and American literature. He is a professor of English at the University of Kansas.

Preface

"Blackmore is himself—of course," said Joseph Conrad, whose evasive remark contains an insight and a warning.[1] For better or worse, the author of *Lorna Doone* is himself, and any account of his career must acknowledge his uniqueness. In an attempt to deal with the man, this study begins with a chapter on his life and keeps referring to his letters in the chronological survey of his work. Though Blackmore wanted no biography, W. H. Dunn published an informative one in 1956, and since then new sources of biographical detail have come to light. These include his correspondence with two major Victorian publishers, his diary for 1855, and a number of unpublished letters collected by the late Professor A. L. Hench at the University of Virginia. The correspondence often clarifies Blackmore's difficulties in writing his novels and sometimes reveals his interpretation of their meaning. The letters also tell something about the way his fiction reflects people and places, though none that I have seen will settle the long controversy over the location of the "real" Doone Valley.

To balance the biographical emphasis, which would have distressed Blackmore, I have related his fiction to other literature, including comparable Victorian novels and the long traditions of pastoral and of romantic comedy in which he usually wrote. As a classicist fond of translating Theocritus and Virgil, he expected to be read in the context of greater authors, and he drew upon Homer and Aeschylus, Aristophanes and Horace as points of reference for his stories. Influenced also by contemporary novelists, he admired the early George Eliot and helped to establish the field of rural fiction in which Thomas Hardy won a longer-lasting fame. To assess his contribution to the rural novel calls for seeing his work in a wide literary perspective. Evaluating his work is always difficult, for Blackmore has unusual powers of giving delight and offense in the same novel. Victorian reviewers both praised and condemned him; Hardy and Robert Louis Stevenson enjoyed parts of his writing, as did another talented and critical admirer, the poet Gerard Manley Hopkins. Even the harsh modern verdict in Ernest Baker's *History of the English Novel* mixes censure with a lament for lost potential: "Blackmore wasted himself . . . on sugary romance and flimsy melodrama, when a man of his literary breeding and genuine talent ought to have done better altogether."[2] But Oliver Elton in 1920 still found him an author of "much life and substance"[3]; W. H. Dunn and Kenneth Budd have praised his achievement in recent decades, and a straggling band of readers has kept alive an interest in more of his works than *Lorna Doone*. My own view is that when Blackmore is accepted as himself, as both Victorian and anti-Victorian, conventional and eccentric, he will appear as one of the three finest rural novelists in nineteenth-century England.

In surveying his uneven achievement, I have depended much upon the critical common sense of Kenneth Budd and the early study by Quincy Guy Burris. Dunn's book provides the main source of biographical information; certain errors in his account have been corrected with facts kindly supplied by the Rev. Michael Hancock, Vicar of Culmstock, and by Mr. A. B. Blackmore, who was in turn indebted to Mr. Douglas Blackmore for details about the career of the novelist's father. Special thanks also go to Dr. T. I. Rae of the National Library of Scotland, Dr. Edmund Berkeley of the University of Virginia Library, Mrs. Margaret Westcott of the Westcountry Studies Library, Mr. Trevor Falla of the Devon Record Office, Mr. G. J. Paley of the Devon and Exeter Institution, Miss Vera Ledger, F .S. A., the librarians at the University of Kansas and the University of Exeter, and to helpful colleagues in Victorian studies at the University of Kansas, including W. D. Paden, George Worth, Harold Orel, Peter Casagrande, and Roy Gridley, and a former colleague and office-mate, Edwin Eigner. I wish also to thank Mr. John Yeowell, the American Philosophical Society, the University of Kansas, which gave two sabbaticals and grants in support of the project, and the editors of *Nineteenth-Century Fiction* and *English Literature in Transition,* who granted permission to reprint parts of two earlier essays in Chapters 3 and 4. I thank my wife Claire for much help with the manuscript and Stephen, Julia, and Katie for encouragement and forebearance in the heart of Devon. Finally, my thanks go to the Rev. and Mrs. Alan Croft and to everyone who was so good to us in Cheriton Fitzpaine.

Chronology

1825   Born June 7 at Longworth, Berkshire, and christened Richard Doddridge, the third son of the Rev. John Blackmore and Anne Basset Knight Blackmore. The first son had died in infancy. Mrs. Backmore died of typhus in October.

1837 -
1843   Attended Blundell's School, Tiverton.

1843 -
1847   Attended Exeter College, Oxford.

1849   Admitted to the Middle Temple, London, to study law.

1852   Called to the bar and began work in London as a conveyancer.

1853   Secretly married Lucy Macguire, November 8 in London.

1854   Anonymously published his first two volumes of poetry.

1855   Published without success his third anonymous volume of poetry and began duties as a master of classics at Wellesley House Grammar School, Twickenham.

1857   Received a legacy enabling him to purchase sixteen acres at Teddington for a new house, orchards, and gardens.

1862   Anonymously published his translation of the first two books of Virgil's *Georgics*.

1864   Anonymously published his first novel, *Clara Vaughan*.

1866   Published *Cradock Nowell*.

1869   Published *Lorna Doone*.

1871   Published his complete translation of Virgil's *Georgics*.

1872   Published *The Maid of Sker*.

1875   Published *Alice Lorraine;* became involved in litigation following the death of his estranged brother, Henry Turberville.

1876   Published *Cripps, the Carrier*.

1877   Published *Erēma*.

1880   After harsh reviews of *Erēma*, recovered his reputation as a novelist with *Mary Anerley*.

1881   Published *Christowell*.

1884   Published *The Remarkable History of Sir Thomas Upmore,* a satire on Darwinism and Liberalism.

1887   Published *Springhaven.*

1888   Mrs. Blackmore died of pneumonia, January 31.

1889   Published *Kit and Kitty.*

1894   Published *Perlycross.*

1895   Published *Fringilla,* his last volume of poetry.

1896   Published *Tales from the Telling House,* a collection of four short stories.

1897   Published *Dariel,* his last novel.

1900   Died January 20, after a long illness, at Teddington.

CHAPTER 1

The Fruit-Grower and Novelist

I was launched into this vale of tears on the 7th of June 1825, at Longworth in Berkshire. Before I was four months old, my mother was taken to a better world, and so I started crookedly. [1]

RICHARD Doddridge Blackmore was not at ease with his own times. Looking back toward his crooked start in 1825, the seventy-year-old novelist could see a life of trials: a childhood without a permanent home, followed by attacks of epilepsy since his schooldays, four decades of growing fruit without profit, and recent grief over the death of his frail wife. Yet his friends drew "a sense of confidence and repose" from his "gentle and placid character," [2] and his novels—for all their violence—always ended happily. Partly because he maintained a hopeful outlook in spite of trouble, he was labeled "the last Victorian" by Kenneth Budd in 1960 in the most recent book on his work. But he also earned the title by being at odds with the times, like Thomas Carlyle, whom he disliked, or John Ruskin, who died in 1900 on the day of Blackmore's death. According to one acquaintance, the novelist belonged by temperament to the eighteenth century, and he described his own as "a far more deeply wicked age of delicate hypocrisy." Elsewhere he called it "a prostituted age." [3]

He was born on the eve of the Victorian era, almost fifteen years after Dickens and Thackeray. Among the great writers born in his own decade were Tolstoy, whose *War and Peace* appeared in the same year as *Lorna Doone*, and Dostoyevsky, with whom Blackmore shared the affliction of epilepsy, a strong nationalistic spirit, and a hatred of socialism. His British contemporaries included the "sensation" novelist Wilkie Collins; the writer of fairy tales and adult fantasies, George MacDonald; and George Meredith, one of Blackmore's few Victorian rivals in ornate eccentricity of style.

13

Fifteen years his junior was Thomas Hardy, the only novelist of the period to surpass him in depicting the rural life of southwestern England.

Though not in the West Country, his birthplace was appropriately rural. The village of Longworth lies below Oxford in the Thames Valley, north of the Berkshire Downs and that strange spot at Uffington where the White Horse gallops in chalk outline along the top of a grassy hill. But Berkshire was next to exile for the novelist's father, the Rev. John Blackmore, born in 1794 at High Bray near Exmoor, where men named John or Richard Blackmore had farmed since at least the seventeenth century. His own father, a clergyman also named John, was rector of Oare and Combe Martin, and had purchased the right to the living at Charles, just south of High Bray and east of Barnstaple. Normally this position would have gone to the older son, the curate of Longworth, but for some unexplained reason it was destined for the younger son instead. His father's decision left John Blackmore a curate all his life, though eventually he would inherit family lands in North Devon.

He had come to Longworth in 1820 as a fellow of Exeter College, Oxford. In the village, he could supplement his small income by "coaching" students for their examinations while carrying out the duties of a conscientious and devout parish priest. Eventually he became a noted preacher, winning praise from a reviewer who hoped that a volume of his sermons might be published;[4] and he was energetic, active in building a new village school and restoring the church later in his career at Culmstock. His future must have seemed promising in 1822 when he married Anne Basset Knight, a distinguished vicar's daughter whose ancestors included a judge under James I, Sir John Doddridge; the nonconformist minister and hymn-writer of the eighteenth century, Philip Doddridge; and Cecil Turberville, the eighteenth-century heiress of Newton Nottage, Glamorganshire, on the south coast of Wales.[5] (Adopted by the novelist's strange elder brother, the Turberville name would figure in a scandalous libel suit in 1875 - 76 before returning to the public eye in Hardy's *Tess of the d'Urbervilles*.) The couple were married at the old Turberville estate on 2 February 1822, and the place became the focal point of their sons' early childhood.

At Longworth, their first son, John Robert Doddridge, was only seven months old when he died in 1823.[6] Henry John was born in 1824 and Richard Doddridge on June 7 of the following year. That summer Mrs. Blackmore's twin sister, Harriet Mercy Knight, came to Longworth to help care for the baby and his year-old brother. By September, typhus was in the house, killing the servants, the doctor, and two of the curate's pupils. Harriet died on September 19; Mrs. Blackmore, on October 4. The baby boy and his brother were placed in the care of another aunt, Mary Frances Knight, and sent to Nottage Court in Wales. John Blackmore wrote the epitaphs for his wife and her sister and penciled in one for himself, leaving blanks for the parish and the year.[7] In 1826 he left the place of his loss to become curate of Bushey in Hertfordshire. There, after five years, he married Ann Platt, the daughter of another clergyman, and was soon rearing a second family. Meanwhile Richard's journey through life had begun—"crookedly."

The impact of his loss was softened by the kindness of his Aunt Mary, who took the children with her to Elsfield Rectory, near Oxford, after her marriage. She was "better than an angel," Blackmore said.[8] His father wrote, "I *know* Mary Knight—in heart she is of all others most like my dear boys' own Mama, & her whole character beautifully exemplifies the spirit of the Gospel. . . ."[9] But as the boys went from parsonage to parsonage in rural Devon, Glamorganshire, and Oxfordshire, they were virtually without a father. John Blackmore was hard-pressed for travel money to see the "poor dear little fellows" in Wales in 1827, and he scarcely could have been more than a friendly visitor to them until after his remarriage in 1831. He left Bushey in December 1832 to return to North Devon as curate of Kings Nympton, bringing his new wife and their infant son, who died only a few weeks after their arrival. Richard probably stayed with his Aunt Mary Gordon at Elsfield until later in 1833, when he was enrolled at Squier's Grammar School in South Molton,[10] about four miles from Kings Nympton. Still later in 1833, he and his brother were moved again, this time to King's School, Bruton, near the eastern edge of Somerset. The boy's wish for a home is expressed in his earliest surviving letter, written to his Aunt Mary during the holidays at Kings Nympton, 13 January [1834]. About King's School he said, "I do not like it at all. It is seventy-seven miles from here."[11]

The distance was lessened in May 1835, when John Blackmore became curate of Culmstock in East Devon, where he served at seventy-five pounds a year until 1841, before moving on to Tor Mohun at Torquay, and finally to Ashford in North Devon, his curacy from 1845 until his death in 1858. At Culmstock he was occupied with his increasing family and the last stages of remodeling the church, while trying to reach the poor in a rural parish with high unemployment and ugly signs of social unrest. Even the "Singing Choir" was causing trouble, after years of playing instruments from the gallery like the Mellstock Choir in Hardy's *Under the Greenwood Tree*. They had quarreled and separated into two factions shortly before John Blackmore's arrival in 1835, and now he appealed for money to buy a barrel-organ as a means of drawing people back from the Methodists. [12] Always seeking funds for worthy causes, he led the victorious campaign for a new school building across the street from the churchyard, winning permission at the same time to take down most of "the old shambles or open air markethouse" along the churchyard wall: now unused, it had become "quite a nuisance as a place of rendezvous for the noisy and dissolute young people of the village on dark & rainy evenings." [13] With so many projects, the curate would have had little time for the two schoolboys, Henry and Richard, who on holidays might have wished to investigate the old markethouse for themselves.

Across the street in the rambling whitewashed parsonage, Mrs. Blackmore was busy raising her four small children (one of whom died in 1835) while keeping an eye on the moral development of her stepsons. Blackmore later called her "a genuine stepmother," without any "womanly weakness, & with lots of splendid cant." From the safety of thirty years afterwards, he said that she was "a blessing to a small boy rather bumptious," but he would not put her in a novel for fear of offending her children. [14] Her character survives most vividly in the letter of 1834 in which she justifies sending her stepsons away to school: "home correction . . . destroys the finer feelings . . . and yet, without correction, boys cannot be educated. Our little Jane evinced some symptoms of self-will, when much younger, but I am thankful to add, by not yielding to her little pets, it is wonderfully subdued; indeed she is now a sweet-tempered baby." [15] The last point indicates the firmness of Mrs. Blackmore's character, for little Jane only would have been in the first self-willed months or weeks of infancy "when much younger."

The forgotten shock of their mother's death and their shifts from place to place were bound to affect the two boys. The story of their loss became part of the sense of identity for the novelist who felt sorry for all motherless "unfledged things." [16] In fiction, he expressed this feeling by depicting characters who have lost at least one parent. Though an orphaned Jane Eyre or David Copperfield or Henry Esmond is a hallmark of the Victorian novel, Blackmore treats the motif with a violence and a persistence that suggest a direct awareness of how life could be shaken by an early disaster. His first three novels begin with the deaths of parents: one father is shot and another is stabbed; a woman dies in childbirth. The effect on the child is shown briefly in *Perlycross* (1894), a novel built from Blackmore's memories of his father at Culmstock. The curate's wife has fallen to her death, leaving her little boy, who saw it happen, "so dazed and daunted . . . that the children of the village changed his nickname from 'Merry Michael,' to 'Mazed Mikey.'"[17] Even where the mind stands the shock, the threat to the child's identity still lingers. The heroine of *Mary Anerley* (1880) states the problem as she sympathizes with a homeless young outlaw: "How very very lonesome it must be for you . . . to have no one belonging to you by right, and to seem to belong to nobody. I am sure I cannot tell what ever I should do, without my father, or mother, or uncle, or even a cousin to be certain of."[18] Her words spell out the theme expressed through the motif of the orphan or the child of unknown parentage. At the same time, they reflect a need for the stability that Blackmore found through his devotion to his wife, aunts, uncles, and cousins, and to the little orchard at Teddington where he lived for the last forty years of his life.

Surrounded by clerical uncles, the boy gave early promise of studiousness, with family legend affirming that at five he was discovered in bed reading the weighty and unillustrated *Edinburgh Review*. At eight he reported going through "the Latin grammar twice," beginning the Greek grammar, and winning a prize book containing "the lives of Hercules and Theseus."[19] He ranked ahead of his older brother at King's School; by the time he entered Blundell's at Tiverton in 1837, he would have been adept at translating Latin verse and able to make his way in Greek. As he advanced to the upper forms at Blundell's, he was set such tasks as the composition of a Greek ode on Hercules or a Latin one on the marriage of Queen Victoria. He was asked to memorize long passages from Virgil and Homer, and on Speech Days he declaimed verses by Milton and Collins, winning the prize in 1842 and 1843. His notebook for 1842 contains Latin translations of Shakespeare and of the striking new poet Alfred Tennyson, whose "Lotos-Eaters" appealed to the hard-working schoolboy. He also took copious notes on the Gospels, commenting on their simplicity of style, a quality usually lacking in his own narratives.

Though he became head boy, his school successes were offset by certain trials, including a nickname which the author of *Blundell's Worthies* considered "too brutally frank" to print.[20] Harder ordeals were the traditional bullying by the older boys and the fighting in which the clever "quiet little fellow" was "very much knocked about."[21] A schoolmate recalled finding him once in bed, his "face swoln and discoloured by a recent combat,"[22] and Blackmore remembered coming home from Tiverton to teach a Sunday-school class "with traces of two very black eyes after a desperate battle." As he entered Culmstock, he met the village schoolmaster, William Jacobs: " 'Been in the wars, Master Richard'—he said (with a wink of secrecy). . . . I was in a fright that he wd draw my father's notice to it while I was inculcating Christian doctrines! But no, he was too much of a gentleman for that."[23]

During his first two years at Tiverton, he boarded with Frederick Temple, the future Archbishop of Canterbury, who once mentioned hitting the author of *Lorna Doone* on the head with a brass hammer. The archbishop found the memory amusing, but according to one account, Blackmore "detested that sort of victimisation, and detested Temple, not only then, but always."[24] At the time, the boy was confronting a worse problem in the form of his first attacks of epilepsy. Blackmore called the disease "the bane" of his life, ever since his "school days,"[25] but as a writer he tried, like Dostoyevsky, to explore the experience and turn it to good account in fiction. Some of his characters endure the ordeal of falling into "the depths of death"[26] through a seizure, and many make symbolic passages from apparent death to new life. Straining the reader's credulity, these little resurrections seemed real enough to an author who knew the experience at first hand: "There is no power of describing it. Those who have been through it cannot tell what happened to them. Only this we know, that we were dead and now we live again."[27] A schoolboy's misery thus provided a personal basis for the archetype of romantic comedy—the pattern of loss and recovery, death and renewal that informs all his major fiction.

Blackmore's career at Blundell's ended with disappointment when he failed to receive the Balliol scholarship to Oxford. It was awarded to a student from Tiverton; so instead of attending Balliol, where Matthew Arnold was still in residence, he entered Exeter College on 7 November 1843 and received the Gifford scholarship the following year. At Oxford he seems to have been unshaken by the Tractarian controversy that divided Anglicans while John Henry Newman prepared to join the Church of Rome. Already as an undergraduate, Blackmore probably disliked change too much to consider such a move, but he soon had reason for avoiding the other extreme of anti-Catholic bias. In the most unconventional and the least documented episode from this obscure period of his life, he fell in love with an Irish Catholic, Lucy Macguire, during a reading party on the Isle of Jersey, and married her secretly after his graduation. Though she became an Anglican, Blackmore was perfectly content that his beloved nieces should be baptized as Roman Catholics.[28] Lorna Doone, after all, was raised a Catholic; a kindly French priest aids a young Englishman in *Springhaven* (1887); in *Alice Lorraine* (1875), an impulsive British officer in Spain doffs his cap to a sculptured saint, saying, "Our family was Catholic for five hundred years; and I don't know why we ever left it off."[29] In a novel about Oxford in the 1840s, *Cripps, the Carrier* (1876), Blackmore pokes fun at the Tractarians rather than at Roman Catholicism. Distinguishing himself from these "Ritualists," he said, "I contend for simplicity, they for trivial complexities."[30] To him, the high Anglicans were the innovators, starting practices which he compared to a puppet show, a "weak sham of Papistry."[31] However uncomplimentary the phrase may sound to the Roman Church, its thrust is against what he considered a new-fangled imitation of an authentic way of worship.

If religious controversy could not disturb Blackmore's love of Oxford, neither could examinations, those times in which a man might be "weighed/ As in a balance," according to Wordsworth, and found wanting. He prepared by studying for such questions as, "What is the leading idea in the History of Herodotus," or "What may be supposed to be the object with which the sins of eminent saints are set before us in Scripture"; he tried to learn the distinction between "the Induction of Aristotle, & that of Modern Philosophy," with the corollary task of "shewing that sometimes one or two particulars are as good as a thousand."[32] Despite his preparations, he failed to win the First in Classics that would have led to a fellowship and a scholarly career. Receiving a Second with his B.A. in December 1847, he faced the future with no clear prospects before him.

The obvious career would have been in the church, but like his older brother he broke family tradition by refusing to become a clergyman. Referring later to his father's piety, Blackmore said, "I never took after him in his strong religion, partly because of pressure."[33] For a year after graduation, he stayed in or near Oxford, coaching a wealthy student "who was looked upon as hopeless."[34] Then deciding to study law, he went to London and was admitted to the Middle Temple on 27 January 1849. Here he met Arthur Joseph Munby, the first of his literary friends. Munby was a poet who moved on the perimeter of Dante Gabriel Rossetti's circle; working-women were his special fascination, and he eventually married, secretly, a former kitchen maid. Blackmore reviewed his friend's poetry in 1852, and he was pleased later in life when Robert Browning also praised it: "The first piece of judgment he has ever displayed. His works make me doubt my own sanity. . . ."[35] Through Munby, the time at the Middle Temple became an introduction to the world of letters, as well as a means of learning enough law to complicate the plots of a dozen novels.

Blackmore was called to the bar in 1852, the year of his M.A. from Oxford, and he began work as a conveyancer, a job that entailed drawing up legal documents without ever having to appear in the courtroom, where he feared an attack of epilepsy. His scanty income from this profession was another reason for shielding relatives from the news of his marriage to Lucy Macguire at Trinity Church, Holborn, 8 November 1853. Not only had she been a Catholic, but her family was Irish and she apparently brought little or no money to the marriage. The match was imprudent, with the bridegroom so unsettled in his profession that he indentified himself as a "writer for the press."[36] Perhaps he was thinking of a few reviews in provincial newspapers or of the poems that he planned to publish in the months ahead.

The couple stayed at Rochester Square, Camden Town, northeast of Regent's Park, while Blackmore prepared two small volumes of poetry for publication. *Poems by Melanter* appeared in May 1854, while *Epullia* came out late in the year with a last-minute poem on the Battle of Alma to catch the public eye in the first exciting months of the Crimean War. But no one paid much attention, and the few reviews were at best condescending. Still Blackmore persisted until a third volume was ready at the end of the year. Appearing in January 1855, *The Bugle of the Black Sea* also failed, and by late February the poet was instructing his publisher to sell off 500 copies at half price. *Epullia* meanwhile brought him the dubious honor of being called "the most prominent of our anonymous poets" in the *Athenaeum*, where he must have been startled at the reviewer's term "epileptic" to describe his "contortions and feverish violence" of imagery.[37]

A cryptic diary in *Punch's Pocket Book for 1855* gives several glimpses of the young man at this trying and obscure time of his life. The entries document his reading of Defoe, Poe, Thackeray, and the major journals during the year, and show that he kept working at poetry, despite another distressing review in the *Athenaeum* ("Bugle treated with contempt. Rather vexed").[38] Though he spent at least one evening in vain "searching for a new subject for tragedy" (January 5) and the one he started remained unfinished, other poems were completed, shown to relatives, and rejected by magazines, while an essay with a translation of Theocritus actually got into print. Only at the year's end did Blackmore begin his first novel, *Clara Vaughan*, which was not published until 1864, when the vogue of "sensation" fiction caused the still anonymous author to be mistaken for Elizabeth Braddon, the most lurid writer of this new school.

Besides showing the projects of the literary man, the diary records something of the Blackmores' domestic life in their second year of marriage. During the cold January and February, Lucy Blackmore sometimes met her husband on his return from the Middle Temple, and she may have gone skating with him at the park. Not yet the semi-invalid whom most people remembered, she walked the dogs even on a snowy day (March 9) and frequently went to church without her husband, whose main church-going in 1855 was reserved for visits with his clerical relatives. His trips– to his uncle and aunt at Elsfield in January and at Easter, and to the Blackmores in North Devon for fishing and shooting in August and early September—were always made without Lucy. Her absence suggests that the marriage was still secret or that she lacked the confidence to move within his genteel family circle.[39] Characterized by Munby in 1863 as Blackmore's "odd goodhumoured insipid little wife" and by a relative as "a dear little thing with her corkscrew curls,"[40] she was undoubtedly retiring. She often spent half the day in bed, and Blackmore usually spoke for her in his letters, ending one with "Lucy coughs her love." But with her sister Agnes she could assert herself, prompting Blackmore's distressed entry for Sunday, August 12: "Close day. Spoiled by row between Ag. & Ly. about friend of former. Ly. decidedly right, but too strenuous. Try to make peace.—Not till night. Bottle of *so called* Madeira. . . . Dinner. Kidney pudding. See poor Ag. off.—Pipe)." A pipe and *The Times* were essential parts of his ritual for composing himself after a sorely trying day.

The young couple's financial trials were unrelieved by the volumes of unsold poetry, so Blackmore took the practical step of applying for a teaching position at the Wellesley House Grammar School in the West London suburb of Twickenham. Hired by the headmaster, Thomas James Scalé, he began work on 12 March 1855, receiving two pounds a week for conducting classes in Virgil and Horace on Monday, Wednesday, and Friday mornings. The work became full-time on May 10, but the salary was not doubled until November, following earnest complaints to Mr. Scalé. By Michaelmas (September 29), Blackmore's combined earnings from teaching and legal work came to about seventy-nine pounds, his expenses to slightly over seventy-six pounds—a "near shave," as he noted in the diary. The teaching duties were rigorous, but if he grumbled about having to "grind" some "very stupid fellows" repeatedly in Virgil (July 11), he found relief in playing prisoner's base and marbles with the boys and in long after-dinner walks with a friend named Dumas, whom he regularly beat at skittles. Commuting from Waterloo Station to Twickenham proved wearisome, however, and by November he was looking for a house nearer to the school. The strain showed at work on November 12 when he suffered a "sort of semi-fit," though he managed to teach again that afternoon and evening. His health on the whole had held up very well, and the diary ends with a happy note: "No fits this year, unless at Twickenham November 12. . . . Laus Deo."

Blackmore taught at Wellesley School until July 1858 (the last date in his class books), in the meantime moving from Camden Town to Hampton Wick near the grounds of Hampton Court. Here he inherited enough money to change his entire mode of life. His bachelor uncle, the Rev. Henry Hey Knight, died in September 1857, leaving lands in trust for Henry and Richard Blackmore, and £1,000 for each in consolidated bank annuities. The new assets allowed the schoolmaster to begin a new career by purchasing a sixteen-acre plot near the "lion-entrance of Bushy Park"[41] in the quiet village of Teddington. The death of his father in the following year brought additional legacies at a time when he was busy planting orchards and gardens. His hope was to find health and a secure living through the wholesome work of fruit-growing. He may also have had some vision of leading a rural life of letters in the tradition of Virgil and Horace, whom he still translated for his own pleasure. He designed a small study upstairs in his new home, a modest gray brick building of Georgian simplicity which he called Gomer

House, after a favorite dog. Eventually shaded by a "magnificent magnolia-tree," the study windows opened on the world of leaf and blossom that fed his imagination. (A visitor reported that birds came through these windows "at his call.")[42] By the summer of 1863 it seemed to Munby that his friend's existence had grown idyllic: "Found him in his gardens, among (for instance) five acres of strawberry beds: & he took me through his vineries, and fed me on lucious grapes. . . ." The setting seemed perfect for the man whose "gentle and placid character gives one always a sense of confidence and repose."[43]

But the pastoral dream never quite came true. Frost, blight, drought, and low prices kept the orchard from paying. Though his pears and roses blossomed beautifully, the losses in some years reached £600 and eventually came to an estimated total of £20,-000.[44] With wry humor, Mrs. Blackmore told the novelist Hall Caine that "but for the 'profits' from her husband's orchard 'they might live in ease and content.' "[45] Even as an ideal, the pastoral dream was difficult to keep once the railroad came to Teddington. The company took a slice of Blackmore's land and built a station just outside his gates; though trees screened the view, the bumping and rushing of trains could be heard from the lawn. Arriving by train in 1865, Munby found the "place miserably changed and all melancholy now to me: a village awkwardly sprouting into a town. . . ."[46] After losing his strawberry crop in 1868 (a year of lawsuit against the railway), Blackmore wrote that he was "utterly sick" of fruit-growing.[47] Nonetheless, he kept on with it for the rest of his life, ordering new strains of pears, apples, peaches, apricots, and roses, stopping fights between laborers, and fretting over low prices, Free Trade, Gladstone (England's "deadliest enemy"),[48] and dishonest marketing at Covent Garden, where he sometimes sold his own produce in vain efforts to receive a fair price. Nothing could quench his love for his "unfruitful farm."[49]

Gardening was much more to him than an expensive hobby. Pruning a vine or building a garden wall gave him his surest sense of identity. "I have taken to trowel instead of pen," he told his publisher, "and am now what nature made me for, a lyer (not in books) but among potsherds. . . . Anyone looking at my vines would say, 'this is your role my good fellow, stick to it; any ass can write novels. . . .' "[50] His appearance emphasized the orchard-man, not the man of letters. Identifying himself as a "fattish individual on the wrong side of 50 . . . whose hands are never

clean,"[51] Blackmore appeared to his guests as a "farmer-like man"
with a marked "air of rusticity."[52] Dressed in "old brown suit of
gardening clothes," with "sleeves tucked up & a big straw hat on,"
he was potting roses at seventy-two when one visitor described him
as a tall man with a "good round healthy shaven red
face . . . white side whiskers, a long nose & a cheery smile, & a
right pleasant voice." But when the conversation turned to Virgil's
Georgics, the poem of farming which Blackmore translated in what
he thought was his best work, the old gardener insisted that Virgil
"like all agriculturalists spoke & wrote more or less in a melancholy
strain." At the end of each book of the *Georgics* "there was a note
of sadness."[53] That summer Blackmore wrote that forty years of
fruit-growing had "lamed, & floored" him and cleaned him out.
"Pomona may pay for sonnets about her, or even for serenading,
but never for the nuptial vow."[54]

His fourteen novels were published between 1864 and 1897 with
the practical purpose of covering the losses from the orchard.
Written mainly in winter or at night during the pruning and
harvesting seasons, they celebrate rural life in every southern shire
from Kent to Devon except Dorset, which he left to the more knowing hands of the poet William Barnes and later to Thomas Hardy.
Though his books were often praised, only *Lorna Doone* became a
best-seller, and it was rejected by at least three leading magazines
before Sampson Low, Marston, and Company acquired it for an
"offer of nothing," according to Blackmore, who claimed that he
made less than £300 from the book during the first seven years after
its publication. He had been lucky to get over £200 apiece for the
rights to serialize his first two undistinguished novels. Eventually
his masterpiece would bring him over £1,000 a year, and after its
success in the early 1870s he would receive about £600 for each of
two novels published in the prestigious *Blackwood's Magazine*.

Fifty pounds per monthly installment was nearly half of his total
income as a master of classics in 1855 and two-thirds of his father's
annual salary as curate of Culmstock; a farm laborer in Devon at
this time might earn half that much in a whole year. But with increasing fame, Blackmore could spurn an offer of this amount from
the *Cornhill Magazine*, and by 1885 the American firm of Harper's
proposed £100 for each installment of *Springhaven*.[55] For the
copyright of an unfinished novel in 1892, his publishers offered £2,-
200,[56] a large sum, though far from the record £7,000 paid by the
Cornhill for George Eliot's *Romola* and 1,000 less than the largest
amounts paid to Anthony Trollope at the height of his fame in 1869.

But Blackmore continued to worry about money as he approached the end of his career. "The sale of my novels has suddenly dropped almost to the vanishing point," he wrote in 1895, and after growing too ill for gardening or writing he was distressed to think of his last two "barren years" without fresh income.[57]

Besides money, his books brought him recognition as "one of our best English novelists" at a time when George Eliot, Trollope, Meredith, and Hardy were all writing.[58] Hardy praised and visited Blackmore after reading *Lorna Doone* in 1875; later, Robert Louis Stevenson wrote him letters of gratitude from Samoa. Other admirers included the Pre-Raphaelite painter Ford Madox Brown, his old friends Arthur Joseph Munby and Mortimer Collins (an ex-Bohemian who caricatured Swinburne), the veteran novelists Margaret Oliphant and William Black, the young novelists Eden Phillpotts, Hall Caine, and James Baker, and the distinguished paleontologist Sir Richard Owen, an ageing opponent of Charles Darwin. But Blackmore's successes were nearly balanced by vexations. Almost all of his novels received at least one hostile review; his poetry never won acceptance, and his last volume, *Fringilla* (1895), annoyed him with its nude illustrations in the "unnatural style" of William Morris and Aubrey Beardsley, whose art he detested.[59] Even the growing fame of *Lorna Doone* brought him a few stings of exasperation. While infant girls from all over the Empire and the United States were being christened "Lorna," he smarted at the neglect of his other books and was enraged to hear a love scene from his last novel described as a "triumph of vulgarity." The same critic advised him to stop trying to represent "modern men and women."[60]

The last forty years of his private life also brought trials, including the scandal over the death in 1875 of his estranged brother, Henry Turberville, who either killed himself by taking cyanide or was poisoned after changing his will to benefit his fiancée, the daughter of a Yeovil chemist. Blackmore was sued for £3,000 for asserting the second possibility.[61] In his own household, ill health was a chronic guest: spells of numbness in his left side hampered his orchard work, while Mrs. Blackmore became a semi-invalid. On the eve of a Christmas holiday, he reported "basting the meat and laying the table" as if he were content with the job; but the strain of poor health may have added to the Blackmores' difficulties in keeping a servant: "We must have a *good tempered* one, being a little short ourselves."[62]

But their childless marriage was brightened by affectionate nieces and nephews, the children of Lucy's sister Agnes and her Portuguese husband, Alfred Pinto-Leite. Aunt Lucy and Uncle Richard took an active and sometimes domineering role in raising Eva, the eldest child, virtually adopting her and entertaining the rest of the family on weekends at Gomer House. Their own outings were short and infrequent. Blackmore never touched foreign soil, the Isle of Jersey apparently being as close as he ever got to France. But the couple were able to go to North Devon in July 1865, when *Lorna Doone* began taking shape, and to Flamborough in 1877 on their farthest journey, which provided the Yorkshire setting for *Mary Anerley*. At the seaside resort of Bridlington, he affectionately inscribed his latest book for her on one of their last long holidays together.

Mrs. Blackmore's death from pneumonia on 31 January 1888 left her husband "lost and wandering, having nothing to live for."[63] He had nursed her through years of illness, but what filled his mind was her kindness to him: "My dear wife lived entirely for me, & tended me with perpetual care, & we scarcely were asunder a week at a time, & even that only rarely. So you may guess what it is to be so suddenly rent away."[64] He was holding her hand on the winter morning when she died. Now he wrote, "All the spring of my mind seems gone"; "I do not care to do anything except wonder and wander about without aim."[65] Yet within a week of the funeral he was full of concern for his nephew, Manoël Pinto-Leite, who was bitten by a dog after coming to stay with his sister and uncle at Gomer House. Blackmore turned at once from his grief to write reassuring reports to Manoël's father, and in May he interceded for the young man, asking Mr. Pinto-Leite to allow him to stay out until eleven or eleven-thirty on Monday and Saturday nights, "when he generally has engagements, either in Minstrelsy at Hampstead, or with his Cricket-club."[66] By the end of the year the widower was at work on a novel celebrating the faithful love of a young husband and wife who live in a small orchard like his own.

As he recovered from grief, his nieces more than repaid his previous kindness by staying with him at Gomer House. He kept on writing and gardening as long as he could, receiving guests and maintaining a wide correspondence until after 1897, when the pain of blocked bowels and cancer made him feel unfit for company. Weakened by months of insufficient sleep and food, he died of influenza on the day of Ruskin's death, 20 January 1900, and was buried beside his wife in the cemetery at Teddington.

Memorials were placed for him in the little church at Oare that *Lorna Doone* made famous and at Exeter Cathedral, where a committee that included James Barrie, Rudyard Kipling, and Thomas Hardy honored him with a marble tablet and a window representing Jonathan, David, and Samson. Above these exemplars of love, courage, and strength are the smaller figures of Lorna and John Ridd and of the hero and villain, barely distinguishable at such height, in their last struggle at the Wizard's Slough. The story was still at the crest of its fame; and despite the author's years of financial worry, he left handsome bequests of land, stock, and money to his nephews and nieces. Nearly £17,000, his copyrights, and his estate at Teddington went to his favorite niece, Eva Pinto-Leite.[67] Named his sole executrix, she respected his command that no biography be written and kept "sacred & secret" whatever "private & confidential matter" he had committed to her charge.[68] She died unmarried in 1911. The orchard eventually gave way to brick rows of suburban homes, and Gomer House was pulled down in 1939, after most of his fiction had already gone out of print. But visitors to Teddington may still find Blackmore's Grove, Gomer Gardens, and a villa named "Lorna Doone," while as late as 1960 the Rev. Kenneth Budd reported seeing a "few surviving fruit-trees."[69] Whether life also persists in Blackmore's gnarled and branchy stories is the basic question for this study.

CHAPTER 2

More Crooked Starts:
Early Poetry and Fiction

Have you never seen the mighty works of "Melanter" . . . wherein he was
going to win fame, but didn't? Then in truth, you are like the rest of the
world, wiser and happier without them.[1]

B LACKMORE'S poems have always been neglected, and the
chief reason for looking at them now is to see what light they
can throw upon his later work as a novelist. He had published no
fiction by 1854 and 1855, when *Poems by Melanter, Epullia,* and
The Bugle of the Black Sea were fresh from the press of an obscure
printer. Appearing anonymously, these volumes had no extrinsic
claim upon the public mind. Greater matters called for attention.
The Crimean War began in March 1854; the summer brought out-
breaks of cholera and intense patriotic enthusiasm, with the latter
reaching a fever pitch on October 6, when *The Times* mistakenly
announced the capture of the fortified city of Sebastopol. During
the long months of disillusionment before Sebastopol actually fell in
September of the following year, other books than Blackmore's won
public notice. There were new volumes of poetry by Tennyson,
Browning, and Matthew Arnold, a best-selling narrative poem, *The
Angel in the House,* by Coventry Patmore, and new novels by
Dickens, Thackeray, Anthony Trollope, and Charles Kingsley,
whose *Westward Ho!* (1855) caught the martial spirit of the time,
removed it from the disenchantments of the Crimea, and glorified it
in a swashbuckling Elizabethan setting. Blackmore's three little
books were lost in the competition.

In retrospect, these volumes assume the importance of landmarks
along the initial stages of an author's career. They introduce the
symbolic figures and the recurrent patterns of action, the
archetypes, that later help to control the incipient chaos of

Blackmore's sprawling narratives in prose. In subject, the poems mingle the classical and the topical, with translations from the Greek alongside verses on the latest news in *The Times*, while juxtapositions of rural and martial themes reveal a lifelong impulse to celebrate both heroic violence and pastoral repose. Finally, a verse tragedy and two other poems ending in suicide express the darker workings of his imagination—an aspect of Blackmore that may be forgotten because of the sunny endings of his novels. While his pseudonym, "Melanter," is a Grecian play on his own name (*melas*, black; *melanteros*, blacker, black-more), its hint of gloom is borne out by several poems and by the concern with suicide in almost half of his stories.

I *Verses Tragic, Romantic, Military, and Pastoral*

Poems by Melanter opens with a five-act tragedy in verse and prose. It is an ambitious beginning, for very few memorable tragedies had been written in England since Jacobean times, and the "Spasmodic" drama of Blackmore's era (which surely influenced his tragedy of murder, madness, and suicide) was ridiculed almost from the start and survives today mainly through histories of Victorian literature.[2] His "Eric and Karine" is based upon Swedish history, which he probably read in an English translation of a work by Anders Fryxell. In turning to history for a subject, Blackmore illustrates Hall Caine's account of his usual creative process: "Not being naturally a story-teller, though a splendid recorder of stories, he invented very little, and depended largely on fact and memory. I think he told me that for almost everything he had written he had the authority of some original."[3] The model for his tragic hero is Sweden's mad King Eric XIV (1533 - 77), the subject of a later play by August Strindberg, who completed *Eric XIV* in 1899. While Strindberg found in Eric a suggestion of Hamlet, Blackmore left no record of what drew him to the monarch. But the play suggests that he saw parallels between Eric and Othello, if not also between the prince's harsh upbringing and the dislocations of his own childhood.

Like Blackmore, Eric lost his mother as a small child. The king remarried and later turned his affections to his second son, John, leaving the boy oppressed by his stepmother and his lifelong habit of distrust. His troubles could have awakened the sympathies of an author who felt distant from his father and grew estranged from his brother, after a childhood without a permanent home. Although Eric became a brilliant and athletic Renaissance prince, his "unaccountable fits,"[4] distrustfulness, and "fantastic faith in astrology"[5] (a subject dear to Blackmore's eccentric elder brother) were early signs of mental unbalance. Paranoia developed during the young king's struggles against Duke John and the conspiring nobles whom he offended by relying upon a base-born counselor and by planning to marry his mistress, Karine, the daughter of a common soldier. Madness overcame him in 1567. That year he took part in the stabbing of a young nobleman, Nils Sture, and then ran wild in a wood before Karine found him and nursed him to his senses. The king's affliction gave him a tenuous kinship with the poet, who called his madness "an epilepsy that hath foamed with blood."[6] The disease afflicting "Melanter" had long been linked with insanity.

Blackmore deals with the crises of Eric's reign by transposing the murder of Nils Sture to a time after the marriage with Karine. The queen never appears as Eric's mistress, as she does in Strindberg, but only as his good angel, a "flower-girl Majesty" like Lorna Doone and other Blackmore heroines, who comes toward her lover bearing nosegays of sweet-briar and gilly-flowers, her "kirtle pinned/ Brimful of cowslips" (4). Although she is a mother, Eric still sees her as the "maid/ Almost a child" who brought him "sweet wood-flowers, / Wild flowers." She is a cousin to Wordsworth's Lucy, "in Nature's keeping safe"(31).

Her vital love contrasts with the deadly will to power in the king's counselor, Peterson, the astrologer. Like Iago in *Othello*, Peterson creates ruin by poisoning the king's mind against his wife. Madness comes once Peterson convinces him that Nils Sture is Karine's lover. To doubt innocence destroys Othello and almost does the same to Leontes in *The Winter's Tale;* in Blackmore it is a recurrent temptation of the romantic hero. Because Karine reflects Eric's soul, the animating principle of his being, to doubt her faithfulness is to commit what the astrologer calls a "suicide of the mind." Rejected by such doubt, the soul becomes a "widow," barely alive, while

> the body with a monster's strength,
> And eyes that are the hoods of fury's crest,
> Hugs the dull cunning of a double self,
> Or dungeoned, gnaws its flesh and pets its shakles. (22 - 23)

By accepting Peterson's whorish image of the queen, Eric gives up his last hold on sanity and becomes the monster who commits murder. Later he regains enough insight to compare himself to the Emperor Nero,

> that vampire butterfly,
> That sheep-eyed, smiling, toying, kissing cut-throat,
> Who knew not—e'en from incest—if he were
> A boy or woman, only not a man. . . . (45)

Split into a "double self," the king has lost his sense of human identity.

The play could end with the tragic hero's recognition of the wreckage within and around him. But Blackmore attempts to transcend tragedy. Before dying, Eric recovers wholeness through his reunion with Karine, whose image heals the split in his psyche. She sings to him of the anima, the feminine image of the soul which his madness could not quite destroy:

> Yon high moon doth forsake
>   Tidal sea and billow,
> And hath in this one lake
>   Mirror and pillow.
>
> So, love, gaze on me,
>   From bright youth to dim age;
> And herein thou shalt see
>   Peace and thine image. (58 - 59)

Her song consoles him, and the couple die blissfully together, drinking the poison that the new monarch has ordered for his imprisoned half-brother. A distortion of history, since Karine lived a long and virtuous life after Eric was poisoned, the ending is too triumphant for tragedy. The dying king enters "realms where everywhere is home" because Karine awaits him with "yet sweeter love" (65). His exit from this realm lacks tragic isolation and silence. It swells instead with the notes of a pre-Wagnerian *Liebestod*.

The mingling of love and death also occurs in what the *Athenaeum* called Blackmore's "serio-comic" translation of "Hero and Leander" by the Greek poet Musaeus.[7] Hero causes her lover's death by luring him to swim the Hellespont on a night of winter storm; when the sea gives up his body, she leaps from her tower to die beside him. The same end is barely averted in another romantic narrative from *Epullia*. In "Lyril Mohun," based on a Devonshire legend of the English Civil War, the heroine sends her lover on a quest to free King Charles from prison, and the young man is lost at sea. But this time the archetype of rebirth governs the action, as it does in Blackmore's prose romances, and the girl revives her lover when he is washed ashore three days afterwards. In "Lita of the Nile," a narrative indebted to Book II of Herodotus, the roles are reversed, with an Arab warrior riding to the rescue just as the priests are about to sacrifice a maiden to the flooding river.

Blackmore thought enough of this poem to include it, carefully revised, in *Fringilla* forty years later. Neither version achieves distinction, but the author's care for the text is one sign that the poem represents an action that haunted his imagination. Lita is the archetypal flower-maiden at the mercy of a dark natural force, the Nile personified as a monster "who swalloweth his bride."[8] Thus far her role parallels the mythic one of Persephone, the goddess of spring whom Hades carries off to become his bride in the underworld. The bride of death reappears in Blackmore's fiction: during the great winter, Lorna Doone faces a threatened wedding with the powerful villain; wearing their bridal robes, the heroines of *Alice Lorraine* and "Frida" both attempt suicide by drowning. In the last two stories and the three poems, water is the destructive element awaiting the bride. Enacting their sacrifice along the bank of the Nile, the priests assume man's bondage to nature: the river brings fertility at the price of a maiden's death.[9] But romance has a way of challenging this assumption. Love breaks the bondage to the natural cycle when the warrior rides to the rescue. This sort of thing can be dismissed as a trick of melodrama (which it is), but it implies one of Blackmore's beliefs about reality. Basically, his belief is that grace works in the world with the power to deliver life from death. Who should object if grace comes charging in on a snow-white horse?

A romantic imagination seeks heroes, and it was Blackmore's lot to belong to an era when these creatures seemed to be an unusually rare and endangered species. Any backward look toward Trafalgar and Waterloo only heightened the contrast with the counting house and the safe Victorian parlor.[10] But the outbreak of the Crimean War charged the air with a promise of glory. In London preparing his volume of patriotic verse, *The Bugle of the Black Sea* (1855), Blackmore was one among millions of young Englishmen for whom the "terrible realities" of war were only "printed words."[11] Ignorance could not stop him from adding more words of his own. Stirred by W. H. Russell's reports in *The Times*, he adopted the viewpoint of a soldier on the battlefront and tried to make poetry from the daily paper. The result, according to the *Spectator,* was "too often little more than a paraphrase of the newspaper correspondence";[12] the fact is that the poems generally lack the interest of Russell's prose.

Poetic diction allowed Blackmore to gloss over too many realities. From the safety of the Inner Temple or Rochester Square, he was still more able than Russell to sustain the British tradition of "elevating" war in language that transforms wasteful and stupid actions into exploits of heroism.[13] Like Tennyson, he wrote a poem on the charge of the Light Brigade. His "Charge of Death" turns the rash attack into an affair of honor: long restrained from action, the proud cavalrymen want a share of fame in the "tournament of death"; their "outraged valor pants to die."[14] After endowing his heroes with this sickly romantic death-wish, he lacks the perception to do anything but glorify it:

> Enough that, in that legion'd mass,
>   They bore their death-crowns through and through,
> And clove with steel the crimson pass
>   Unto the only rest they knew —
> The rest of brave men's outraged fame,
> When glory weeps to write their name,
> And nations all too late confess
> Their truest pride is their distress. (103)

As in Tennyson, a blunder becomes a source of national self-esteem.

Personification is the special vice of Blackmore's war poetry. In "The Battle of Alma," British "pluck and thew" join with providence to win glory, a "tearful bride"; "valour" strides forward against the "Dragon" Czar Nicholas in "The Bold March." Poetic figures keep obscuring the subject, even when the author confesses his inability to deal with it:

> Too well I know, how weak my puny hand
> (So tremulous even in the lap of peace)
> To grasp the gauntlet of unlettered War

—a being who nonetheless "hath a heart" beneath his armor ("Overture"). Altogether, *The Bugle of the Black Sea* represents the peril of treating matters beyond one's experience and understand-

ing. Blackmore made better sense about the subject when he glanc-
ed at it indirectly in a poem having nothing to do with the Crimea:

> Alas, we love not peace aright;
> We make no inmate of our rest,
> But only treat her as a guest,
> For whom we mean to fight.[15]

The theme of peace reveals another impulse in the poet of sabers,
rescues, and tragic madness. Despite his thirst for heroism, he was
also drawn toward pastoral repose. The opening of a bud or the
ripening of fruit could content him with sufficient action. Pastoral
moments come in the poems of war, as in the pause before the Battle of Alma when a "gleaner child" walks by with sheaves upon her
head. From reports of how British soldiers gorged themselves on
grapes and peaches in one valley, Blackmore creates a long pastoral
interlude, omitting the fact that many of the men became deathly
ill from overeating. Violence grows calm before a rose-hung cottage
in "The Bold March," and soldiers who in reality looted the
pastoral valley stand charmed by two maidens playing upon harps.
For the moment, the heroic impulse vanishes at the thought of
"home": "Once speak that magic word,/ What becomes of
glory?"[16]

Blackmore's early pastoralism comes out most clearly in his
translations of Theocritus and Virgil. In the midst of the war, he
published "Sicilian Hours," a little essay with his translation of
Theocritus's Idyll VIII, and he stepped forward as an advocate of
tranquillity: "To induce the British public, in its present warlike
mood, to rest a few minutes beneath a hedge, and hear a shepherd
sing, would be a triumph greater than any we seem like to
gain. . . . And yet, I do desire that one or two may turn aside with
me, and help me to recall, and render to our English lanes, a song in
other tongue and time so passing sweet; nor am I without an argu-
ment or two to convince those willing to believe, that a little quiet
may stand them in good stead."[17] He was introducing the
shepherd's song which later became the epigraph for *Lorna Doone:*

> None of Pelops' land for me—
> Not for me a purse of gold,
> Nor than winds more swift to be!
> Only in my arms to hold
> Thee, and sing to bevied sheep,
> Grazing toward Sicilian deep.

These lines would express the pastoral values underlying and counterpointing the story of romantic heroism upon Exmoor.

Theocritus, his "favourite poet,"[18] and Virgil rivaled Shakespeare in claiming Blackmore's highest literary allegiance. Translating the *Idylls* and the *Georgics* was both a discipline and a recreation, and this work became a form of preparation for writing novels about the English countryside. As models, the *Idylls* and the *Georgics* are complementary, with the first dwelling on rustic leisure, while the second describes the labor of raising grain, fruit, and livestock, and of tending bees. Both link the little events of rural life with the cosmic order of religious celebration and seasonal change, as Blackmore would do in his pastoral fiction.[19] The harvest supper in Idyll VII, the reapers' song in Idyll X, and the ceremonies before reaping in the first *Georgic* have their West Country equivalents in the harvest chapter of *Lorna Doone*, which carries on the festive spirit of its classical models. Although neither Theocritus nor Virgil pictures rusticity as bliss, both could encourage Blackmore to look to the countryside for images of the good life. He must have nourished a dream of idyllic love in a garden ever since his adolescent study of *Paradise Lost*, for the dream recurs in two early poems based on legends of Adam and Eve[20] and in the flowery love-scenes of his fiction. A humorous version of it comes out in his portrait of the Virgilian "happy farmer" in his first novel, *Clara Vaughan*. The brawny Devonshire wrestler Jan Huxtable and his cheery wife have so fruitful a farm, so rich a store of butter, clotted cream, bacon, and cider, and so many young children that their home becomes something like a seedbed for fresh life in a story of murder and revenge. Huxtable's prototype comes directly from Virgil, near the end of the second Georgic, translated here by Blackmore:

> Sweet children cluster round the farmer's kiss,
> The chaste home keeps the innocence of bliss,
> The cows stand full of milk, and on the grass
> Fat kids cross horns, to try a sportive pass.
> The farmer, in the midst, keeps holiday,
> And, while his co-mates crown the bumpers gay,
> Beside the bonfire, stretch'd upon the sod,
> Invites and pledges thee, O Vintage-god!
> Marks elms for targets to his shepherds' aim
> And bares their muscle for the rustic game.[21]

The two farmers are much alike, except Huxtable, like John Ridd in *Lorna Doone*, would be baring his own limbs for the bout of wrestling.

With their pictures of the good rural life, Theocritus and Virgil provide details of the countryside that any disciple must learn to observe. Theocritus records the sound of insects in the noonday heat and imitates rustic speech in the Doric dialect. Blackmore followed his example, while denying that Devon speech was at all "Doric";[22] more immediate models for representing local dialects included Robert Burns, Sir Walter Scott, George Eliot, and the Dorset poet William Barnes, to whom he was compared in a review of his second novel,[23] and whose work he must have noticed at the time in *Macmillan's Magazine*. If growing up in rural Devon, Wales, and Oxfordshire provided a background for imitating rustic speech, working as a gardener and orchard-man further qualified Blackmore for pastoral writing. To translate the *Georgics* was almost like studying the manual for his daily tasks—one written by a poet with his own passion for noting weather-signs and describing great storms. Having done the job himself, he could appreciate Virgil's instruction for budding and grafting:

> Nec modus inserere atque oculos imponere simplex.
> nam qua se medio trudunt de cortice gemmae
> et tenuis rumpunt tunicas, angustus in ipso
> fit nodo sinus; huc aliena ex arbore germen
> includunt udoque docent inolescere libro.
> aut rursum enodes trunci resecantur et alte
> finditur in solidum cuneis via. . . . (Bk. II, 11. 73ff.)

Blackmore's translation gives a vivid account of the two delicate processes:

> Nor is the mode to bud and graft the same—
> For where the buds, (like emeralds in their frame,)
> Push'd forth the bark, their filmy jerkins split,
> A narrow eyelit through the crown is slit;
> Herein the germ, a stranger, they compress,
> And teach with juicy rind to coalesce.
> To graft,—the knotless trunks are lopp'd amain,
> And cleft with wedges deep into the grain. . . .

Throughout the passage, he tries to be specific, picturesque, and as faithful to Virgil's unrhymed lines as his cramped couplets will allow. Where a modern translation by C. Day Lewis has "delicate sheaths" for *tenuis tunicas*, Blackmore retains an image of clothing in "filmy jerkins," a more picturesque expression for a bud's close-fitting covering. In a famous earlier version, John Dryden supplies no metaphor of clothes for *tunicas*, though with "shooting Gems" he keeps alive the second meaning of *gemmae*, a word for both buds and gems. Blackmore's "emeralds" is a still more specific noun than the original, and it sustains and colors a metaphor which Lewis altogether ignores. When Blackmore departs from Virgil by using "crown" for *nodo*, he does so to avoid confusion: the literal translation of *nodo* as "knot" in Lewis and Dryden suggests a much larger and woodier swelling than one made by a bud. Blackmore saves the literal equivalent for the place it belongs, rendering *enodes trunci* as "knotless trunks." Whatever his wisdom in deciding to rhyme Virgil, he deserves the *Spectator's* praise for precision in employing "technical terms."[24]

The novelist took more pride in this translation than in any other of his writings. Sharing Virgil's concern for the growth of plants as well as empires, he too sensed a divine power at work in both processes, despite untimely frosts on the one hand and Gladstone on the other.[25] As for Theocritus ("ah I knew that grand fellow by heart almost, once upon a time"),[26] his humor and clarity of vision shine like sunlight through the tangled undergrowth of Blackmore's fiction, while the expert account of a boxing-match in Idyll XXII provides a classic model for reporting the wrestling-bouts in his fiction. But neither poet could give Blackmore the secret for writing great novels. If anything, the *Georgics* might encourage him to write more minutely of pears than of people and to indulge in the horticultural pedantry that weights many of his pages. His habit of constructing a scene as if it were a Theocritan idyll ("eidyllion," a little picture) works against the need to develop a continuous flow of action. The framed parts of a Theocritan novel are apt to be more satisfying than the whole. Blackmore might gain descriptive power from studying Virgil and a feeling for rustic character from Theocritus, but for the supreme task of plotting a novel he needed other models.

II   Clara Vaughan *and* Cradock Nowell

Model plots were bafflingly abundant for an author who admired "the great Defoe,"[27] Dickens, and Thackeray, and considered Bulwer-Lytton "the greatest writer of the century."[28] Significantly, Bulwer-Lytton was the most articulate defender of romantic fiction in an age of realism. Blackmore was drawn toward a tradition that led back to ancient times when it was established by such romancers as Longus and Heliodorus. In *Daphnis and Chloe* by Longus and *The Ethiopica* by Heliodorus, the essential story is of two simultaneous processes: the lovers' struggle to be united and their discovery of who they are. This basic plot could inform works as magnificent as Shakespeare's *Winter's Tale* or as mundane as the latest Victorian melodrama. It could be enlivened by outlaws, abductions, threats of murder and rape, and ordeals through fire or water, as in Mozart's opera *The Magic Flute*. Tested in their initiations, the lovers finally discover their true parentage and unite in marriage. Apparent calamity turns out to be good fortune, and fate becomes providence, suggesting that "there *are* divinities who shape the ends of their special charges."[29] These features, as well as the formal technique of the tale within the tale that is so frequent in Heliodorus, are characteristic of Blackmore's romances. Promising disaster, with quotations from Greek tragedy sometimes on the title page, his stories move from ominous beginnings and acts of violence toward providential ends—the "eu-catastrophe" or good turn of fortune that J. R. R. Tolkien admired in fairy tales and brilliantly created at the climax of *The Lord of the Rings*.

Begun in 1855, Blackmore's first novel was both archaic in its romantic plot and contemporary in its tone and setting. As a weekly serial in a popular magazine, *Clara Vaughan* (called *The Purpose of a Life* in the magazine)[30] seemed like another of the current "sensation novels" in the school led by Wilkie Collins and Elizabeth Braddon in 1864. Their works exist for the sensational moment, such as the apparent visit of a ghost in *The Woman in White* (1860) or the surprising feat of a femme fatale who shoves a man down a well in *Lady Audley's Secret* (1862). Blackmore insisted that his book was finished before the sensation novel became a craze, but *Clara Vaughan* bears the marks of the new thrillers. A sudden ray of sunlight illuminates the initials traced in blood above the bed of Clara's murdered father; as narrator, she must suffer an attack of epilepsy, temporary blindness, and hysteria before confronting an apparent ghost and the murderer himself. The setting has the latest mid-Victorian conveniences: detectives, telegrams, and the railway—Clara catches the train from Paddington Station to Gloucester just in time for the climactic scene. A murder mystery, lurid and topical, *Clara Vaughan* rivals the sensation novels whether Blackmore meant for it to or not.

But it has other dimensions that make it a far less streamlined story than those pantingly told by Miss Braddon. Clara is seen from the beginning against a background of Greek myth. Her prototype is Electra, the daughter of Agamemnon, who seeks with her brother Orestes to avenge her father's death. For both daughters, justice cries, "blood stroke for the stroke of blood/ shall be paid."[31] These lines from *The Libation Bearers*, the second of Aeschylus's plays about the murder of Agememnon, appear on the title page to establish the theme of the novel. Like Electra, Clara seeks justice and understands it as revenge. Her childhood devotion to her father becomes an obsession with vengeance as she grows up into a high-strung, often rash young woman, who finds it difficult to express love. Blackmore does not endow her with a full "Electra complex" (she bears no ill-will toward her mother), but the heavy symbolism of an Exmoor stag marks her first encounter with a young artist[32] and the sexuality that she represses. Throughout the story, most of her caresses are reserved for the artist's sister and their great dog Giudice, whose name identifies the object of her ruling passion.

She gains release from her obsession through a vicarious initiation into romantic love. In a long story within the story, her dying uncle tells of his journey to Corsica, the island of the vendetta, where "law the first" is revenge (253). Clara sees the effects of acting on this law at the same time that she enters vicariously into a world of romantic emotion. For her uncle's story concerns his love for a Corsican girl whom he calls "Lily," another of Blackmore's flower-maidens and one of the few who not only bloom but die. After the abduction of their two small children and Lily's death, the husband is saved from suicide by a sense of her presence, but melancholy leaves him the sinister figure whom Clara in childhood accused of murdering her father. Now she learns the sense in which the accusation was true, only to find the knowledge less important than her new understanding of her uncle's life. Loving him, she begins to accept his counsel: "Leave your revenge to God" (303). After staging his reunion with his lost daughter ("Lily come back from the grave"), Clara prepares for the last of her own ordeals, the confrontation with the murderer.

She passes the test by giving up revenge. The villain's fate is left to the Herculean Farmer Huxtable and the dog Giudice, "a brute beast . . . who wreaks . . . that vengeance for which the desire has died out in the human heart." The critic writing these words in the *Examiner* was the only one, according to Blackmore, who caught the "moral" of the story, and almost the only one to maintain that the novel, "with all its defects," was "unmistakenly a work of original genius."[33] Elsewhere the defects of the plot received more attention. The *Spectator* called it "a tissue of absurdities";[34] the *Athenaeum* summed it up as "ill-constructed, clumsy, and absurd."[35]

The best-liked parts had the least to do with the main story. These were the accounts of the Huxtable family in their North Devon farm near the valley of Trentisoe, some six miles west of Lynmouth. Knowing the neighborhood from childhood, Blackmore was, he said, "thoroughly inborn & ingrained" with "the pith of Devonshire life,"[36] and he put several bits of it into his first novel. Seen through the aristocratic narrator's slightly patronizing eyes, the Huxtable's kitchen holds part of the essential Devon: a huge chimney "podded with great pots and crocks hung on things like saws" and a "floor of lime and sand" worn "into pits such as boys use for marbles" (42 - 43). The room chirps and bubbles with Mrs. Huxtable's North Devon speech—"the only vitty talk," as she tells Clara, who learns "that to 'quilty' is the proper English for to 'swallow,' and that the passage down which we quilty is, correctly speaking, not the throat, but the 'ezelpipe' . . ."(49). Young Sally Huxtable's letters to Clara portray the family from the inside, as in the report of how she saved her brother from "that minx of a Tabby Badcock":

only a week ago last Tuesday I come sudden round the corner, and catched her a kissing of our Jack in the shed there by the shoot. And after all you taught her, Miss! Jack he ran away, as red as a mangawazzle,[37] but that brazen slut, there she stand with her legs out, as innocent as a picture. Never a word I said, but with no more to do I put her head in the calves' stommick as we makes the cheese with, in a bucket handy. It would have done you good to see her, Miss, she did cry so hard, and she smell of it for a week, and it cured our Jack, up to Sunday anyhow. (311)

Here, said the *Spectator,* "the racy vernacular of Devonshire" nearly satisfies "that morbid hunger of the author for showy writing which in other parts of the novel makes the style periodically almost rancid."[38]

A further relief from the stale passages is the characterization of Jan Huxtable, Blackmore's first re-creation of the happy farmer in Book II of Virgil's *Georgics.* Beloved by his wife and their ever-increasing family (nine children before the novel ends), Farmer Jan becomes a figure of local legend, partly from his own strength and partly from the poetic gifts of the parish bard who gives him the Homeric epithet of "Varmer Brak-plew-harnish" after he snaps a trace when pulling his own plough through a field on a wager. The overwrought Clara flourishes among the Huxtables, admires the farmer, and takes time to give a highly expert account of his championship wrestling bout before narrating the climactic scene. There the farmer joins with the great dog Giudice as a force of life against the villain, who not only kills men but subjects dogs to vivisection. The farmer has a symbolic importance in this conflict, but to become a figure of mythic stature he would have to play a larger part in the whole novel. At most he makes a lively comic figure, reminiscent of the kindly blacksmith Joe Gargery in *Great Expectations* (1861). With his wife and his daughter Sally, he provides an earthy balance to the high-flown emotions of sensation fiction. The role of a mythic hero would wait for another Exmoor farmer, the narrator of *Lorna Doone*.

Despite the reviews, Blackmore was proud of his first novel. "I am incapable of better writing," he told the publisher Alexander Macmillan, and later said, "The Corsican episode . . . is better than anything I could write now; when I never can stick to the passions of people, but slip to the ludicrous side of things."[39] But he did face the basic criticism that would follow him throughout his career as a novelist. According to the *Spectator*, he lacked "the power for a closely knitted plot"—a weakness which he realized would prove "fatal . . . to all real success." But was the criticism justified? In brave desperation, he wrote, "What I wd. give for some great true judge to tell me if this be so!"[40] He was appealing to Macmillan, the judge with the power of accepting or rejecting his second novel, *Cradock Nowell*. *Macmillan's Magazine* was one of the two or three most prestigious journals in England for serialized fiction, and Blackmore was eager for a more cultivated audience than the readers of the cheap weekly paper in which *Clara Vaughan* had first appeared. Macmillan accepted the manuscript; Blackmore finished it in April 1865, and *Cradock Nowell* ran in the magazine from May 1865 through August 1866. In his fortieth year, the new novelist was ready for success.

He had chosen his material to please almost everyone. For lovers of nature, the main setting was the New Forest around Lyndhurst and Ringwood,[41] a region wild enough to stir interest yet near enough to London to be visited by thousands of potential readers. Knowing Hampshire only from visits and fishing trips, Blackmore relied upon an illustrated book, *The New Forest: Its History and Scenery* (1863) by John R. Wise, a follower of John Ruskin in the appreciation of natural and architectural beauty. Blackmore pays tribute to Wise midway through the novel, and he must have shared Wise's belief that "beauty is one of the chief ends and aims of nature," as well as his awareness that natural beauty was threatened by industrialization. "The flowers cannot grow in our stony streets," Wise wrote; "the glory of the morning and evening is blotted out by the fog of smoke which broods over our cities."[42] Ruskin, William Barnes, William Morris, and Gerard Manley Hopkins all felt this threat to natural beauty, and they responded not only by complaining but by trying to preserve in words something of the "freshness deep down things" and to inspire readers with the will to protect what was left. For Ruskin and Wise, purple prose was an instrument of ecology, and Blackmore followed both in evoking the lights and shadows of the New Forest through the lattice-work of beeches and oaks.

For contrast, he included detailed scenes among the slums and railway yards of London, as if challenging direct comparison with Dickens, whose latest novel, *Our Mutual Friend*, he was reading while at work on *Cradock Nowell*. As in *Clara Vaughan*, the setting was recent, with the main action occurring in 1859 - 60; Captain Marryat had already written a historical novel called *The Children of the New Forest* (1847), and Blackmore was intent upon showing that he was abreast of his own times. But anyone who loved the classical past could linger over the Latin and Greek quoted by the benevolent country parson, John Rosedew,[43] and folklorists and linguists would find points of interest concerning the legends and dialect of the New Forest. For another sort of readers, scenes at the Nowells' country house might suggest the genteel comedy of Anthony Trollope. Blackmore did not care for Trollope, but at this stage of his career he seemed ready to follow almost any example that might lead to success.

His most important model, however, must have been Henry Kingsley's *Ravenshoe* (1862), a recent popular success in *Macmillan's*. As Malcolm Elwin pointed out in *Victorian Wallflowers*, *Cradock Nowell* shares an almost embarrassing number of motifs with Kingsley's novel. The plots of both turn upon the confusion resulting from the interchange of another baby for the infant heir of an estate—the basis for comedy later in Gilbert and Sullivan, but for much misery in the two novels. In each, the hero comes of age only to learn that he is not the rightful heir, and he leaves the manor house to live under an assumed name among the poor in London. Kingsley's hero states the theme that is implicit in any serious treatment of this situation: "the most terrible agony . . . was the feeling of *loss of identity*—that I was not myself; that my whole existence from babyhood had been a lie."[44] Both novels emphasize the ironies of a social structure that defines a person's value by the accident of birth. The baronet in each novel employs either an illegitimate half-brother or one thought to be illegitimate, and the baronet's son tries to seduce the daughter of his base-born uncle. Growing up in this baffling tangle of kinship, the hero must somehow accomplish a rite of passage through the whole labyrinth of the Victorian caste system. He discovers his basic identity by losing his safe place on a country estate and entering for a time the other realm of shame, poverty, and killing drudgery. Only then can he move on to a responsible role in Victorian society.

Blackmore's "Tale of the New Forest" begins with an epigraph from *As You Like It*, a comedy suggesting the genteel pastoral world of the hero's origins. The narrator will compare his heroines to Rosalind and Celia in the Forest of Arden, and his prose will run riot as he describes their loveliness on a flowery day in spring. But in view of the main action, Touchstone's command, "let the forest judge" (III, ii), also points to the mystery of guilt for the murder of the hero's twin brother. Cradock Nowell's ordeal is to bear his father's blame for the death of the favored son. As Shakespeare's play develops from the ill-will between two sets of brothers, the novel also builds upon this situation. Cradock is thought to be jealous of his brother Clayton, who has recently been named the rightful heir; and their father's illegitimate half-brother has long suppressed his resentment against the baronet. For a myth to express the tragic potential of this conflict, Blackmore went beyond *As You Like It* to Herodotus's story of Adrastus, the young man who by accident killed both his brother and the son of King Croesus before taking his own life. The myth comes into the novel after the heir falls from a gun-shot wound in the forest where Cradock was hunting. Though Cradock escapes conviction for the murder, his father blames him for it, and he leaves in disgrace for London. There he begins a desperate life in the slums as "Charles Newman." After a long nightmare of apparent guilt, illness, thoughts of suicide, temporary insanity, and abandonment off the coast of Africa, he finally awakens with his honor, health, and goods restored. For him, the story of Adrastus becomes only an awful might-have-been.

But for his unacknowledged uncle, Bull Garnet, Adrastus's burden of guilt is more than a bad dream. Garnet shot the young heir for trying to seduce his daughter, and he is left to wrestle with his conscience after Cradock goes away in disgrace. He lashes himself at night by the Murderer's Oak in the New Forest, where the mild-mannered Parson Rosedew stumbles upon the bloody scene: "Garnet a wild flagellant!" says the parson from a discreet distance; "I knew that he was an enthusiast, but not that he was such a fanatic. . . . I must reason with him about it, if I ever find good occasion" (298). Being a man of great tact, Rosedew walks away, leaving Garnet to bear his burden alone for most of the story. When he finally confesses, the baronet's stunned response makes him fear that he has destroyed his half-brother as well as the young heir. He knows now the burden of Adrastus, only the guilt he bears is more directly of his own making.

Intended from the start to be a "leading character" (42), this proud "man of power" comes close to tragic stature. He is something of a forerunner of Michael Henchard in Hardy's *Mayor of Casterbridge*, stubborn like Henchard and at once violent and repressed. But by refusing to present this murderer as a villain, Blackmore offended at least one Victorian critic, who insisted that there be "no more portraits like Bull Garnet."[45] The murderer invites sympathy because the crime springs from his extravagant love for his daughter and from a life-time of stifled resentment against his base birth and the wrong done to his mother. As he breaks under the strain of guilt and worry over his two children, he faces death as a "great blank depth" where "nothing belonged to him any more—only utter, utter loss, and not a chance of heaven" (430). But Blackmore does not let him die in tragic isolation or without the hero's words of reassurance: "May God forgive me as I do you. Wholly, purely, for once and for all!" (449). Forgiveness, a rare act in Hardy's darker fiction, works against the sense of tragedy. At the end of the scene, when the narrator speaks to the reader, his concern is not with the lost possibility of a tragic death but with evading the Victorian demand for poetic justice: "Now, think you not that his man was dying a great deal better than he deserved? No doubt he was. And, for that matter, so perhaps do most of us. Yet who can be blamed for that, but God?" (449).

Near the end, the narrator dreams fondly of a time when his tale will become a legend, as if the story of Adrastus could blend with *As You Like It* and produce a myth of the New Forest. But his next words express a doubt of his success. The "forest-children" of the future should tell the story "more simply, and more sweetly," without going "astray from inborn sympathy. For every grown-up man is apt to mar the uses of his pen with bitter words, and small, and twaddling; conceiting himself to be keen in the first, just in the second, and sage in the third. For all of these let him crave forgiveness of God, his fellow creatures, and himself, respectively" (450). Except for rare persons like Robert Louis Stevenson, who felt "blessed" from reading *Cradock Nowell*, this apology must have seemed long overdue. The novel strays into overelaborate description, sentimental or simply trivial dialogue, and authorial asides; dozens of figures cross its shifting stage in a drama that mingles comedy and melodrama with unkept promises of tragedy. Where Blackmore hoped to achieve the memorable clarity of a legend, he left a blurred Victorian sprawl.

Not surprisingly, the publication of so rambling a work became an ordeal for both the author and Alexander Macmillan. Editorial complaints caused Blackmore to rewrite the ending and later to revise the whole novel for the 1873 edition. "It seems to have been begun by one person, and finished by another,"[46] said a critic who suspected that serialization had caused difficulties. Macmillan published a highly respectable magazine in a highly prudish decade, and he begged the author to stop marring his work with "queernesses and coarseness."[47] Blackmore responded with his most stinging attack upon Victorian prudery—"this sham virginity of a prostituted age." Sick of it, he wrote, "Lo our fashionable ladies, taking their manners from men about town, their talk from livery stables, their air, hair, & dress from kept women . . . would faint, if my hero blows his nose. How can you fail to perceive the rottenness of such refinement?"[48] But Macmillan wished to protect the refined sensibilities of readers who shared the view that "man at his best is a disembodied spirit." At a time when certain agnostics and Platonistic churchmen found something grossly material and coarse in such "primitive" doctrines as "the resurrection of the body and the eucharistic sacrifice,"[49] Macmillan accused Blackmore of Anglo-Catholic tendencies for dwelling so much on physical fact.

The author responded indignantly, denying any connection with the "ritualists," whom he "heartily" despised. He insisted that the

issue was a "question of art": having "to deal with embodied
human life, it is almost essential . . . to allude now and then to it's
[*sic*] outward manifestations."[50] He wanted nothing subversive:
"surely you do not suppose that because I object to a sham refinement, a perpetual consciousness of sexuality, what in fact I may call
a prurient prudery, that I advocate savage nudity." He simply asked for the freedom to mention "a lady's back or bosom" and to
depict characters as frankly as those in Dickens: "None of my people were allowed to spit. In our 'Mutual friend,' there is mutual &
monosyllabic expectoration, over & over again."[51] But for all his
protests, he gave in to Macmillan, just as he would to John
Blackwood in the next decade. Bowdlerized and cut, the novel that
was to prove his success exasperated critics and defeated his own expectations: "If I don't succeed with C. N., I can't succeed with
anything."[52] After *Cradock Nowell*, almost no one was interested in
the manuscript of *Lorna Doone*.

The pity is that so allusive and often vivid a work should be so
nearly unreadable. It contains minute notes of things that should be
remembered—the life of the forest, the gamekeeper's dialect, and
the way a woodcutter's lunch dwindles from leftover bacon on
Monday to bread and potatoes as the week goes by (335). It also
contains three of the most striking descriptive chapters in Victorian
fiction. One shows the baronet's disgraced son trying to survive his
first day as a shipping clerk in a railway yard of the "Grand Junction
Wasting and Screwing Line." Titled "Down Among the Dead
Men" after a popular song, the chapter marks the hero's descent
into a London hell of steam engines and lurching cars "where
danger ran in converging lines, where a man must stand sideways,
like a duellist, and with his arms like a drill-sergeant's, and not
shrink an inch from the driving wheels . . ."(248). In this scene
Blackmore writes more convincingly of heroism than he ever
managed to do in his poems on the Crimean War. To "run in and
out, and through and through, in that perpetual motion, to be
bound to jot down every truck, the cover, and contents of it . . . to
have nobody to help you therein, and nobody to cry 'dead man' if
you died, and the certainty that if you stood a hair's-breadth out of
the perpendicular, or a single wheel had a bunion, you with the
note-book in your hand must flood the narrow 'tween ways, and
find your way out underneath to heaven; all this, and the risk of the
fearful jumps from one sliding train to another, sliding oppositely,
and jerking, perhaps, as you jumped"—this, Blackmore says, "call-

ed for a glorious inglorious courage, grander than any that ever won medal or cross for slaughtering" (245ff.). This time the involved periodic syntax brings home the bafflement of a man in a labyrinth. Ending with an allusion to Charon, the freight-handler of Hades, the passage evokes a hell that greed has built, "all because the Screwing Company would not buy land enough to get elbow-room."

Paralleling this scene of man-made chaos are the two chapters on the great storm of 1859. Heavily overwritten, as if Ruskin were describing another seascape by Turner, the prose becomes alliterative and roughly metrical in the account of two men struggling along the wind-swept beach: "Crusted with hunks of froth and foam-drift, drenched by pelting sheets of spray, deafened by the thundering surf, and often obliged to fly with the wind from a wave that rushed and hissed at them, they battled for that scoop of the bay where the ship must be flung by the indraught" (184). The pounding cadences make the whole episode sound less like the parallel scenes in *David Copperfield* and *Ravenshoe* than Hopkins's later account of a storm in "The Wreck of the Deutschland" (1876). Both the rhythms and the imagery anticipate the poem as the "large ship, swept and naked," comes into view: "Swept of her masts, of her canvas naked; but clad, alas! with men and women, clustering, clinging, cowering from the great white grave beneath them." The phrase for the breaking seas, "the swirling, hurling whiteness" (189), has the close-rhyming force of Hopkins, and both writers use similar images in describing an attempted rescue. Of course, purple prose is no substitute for great poetry. But Blackmore's often has a vigor that outshines the rhetorical bombast, and Hopkins became a devoted admirer of his "wordpainting." As an Oxford undergraduate, he might have read the chapter when it appeared in *Macmillan's* in December 1865.

For the novelist, wordpainting would be wasted until he could construct a coherent narrative around one unifying action. Having failed again in the effort, he tried a third time after a holiday with his wife in North Devon during the summer of 1865. By the following February, he had started *Lorna Doone*,[53] abandoning the Victorian setting of his first two novels for the seventeenth century on the western moors. No longer imitating current best-sellers, he turned instead to legends of Exmoor that were known to him from childhood and perhaps brought to mind by a story called "The Doones of Exmoor," published in the weekly *Leisure Hour* during

September and October of 1863.[54] The result would be not so much another novel as an avowed romance, less dependent upon seeming probable than upon awakening poetic faith. The third time became a charm. The grower of fruit trees and vines at last found a way to represent human growth, from early trauma and later trials, toward faithfulness and love.

CHAPTER 3

The Mythic Appeal of Lorna Doone

Our great walnut lost three branches, and has been dying ever since; though growing meanwhile, as the soul does.[1]

WHAT *Cradock Nowell* failed to do for the New Forest, *Lorna Doone* (1869) achieved for Exmoor: it gave the region a distinctive myth. Almost from the first, the story sent tourists trudging along Bagworthy ("badgery") Water in search of the Doone Valley, as if reading about the place were not quite enough. By 1889, Blackmore's imagined world had grown so real that the Doone Valley appeared on the Ordnance Survey maps, and experts have debated its location ever since. The issue became especially vexed during the centenary of *Lorna Doone* in 1969, when Sir Athol Oakeley tried to persuade the mapmakers that the real Doone Valley was not Hoccombe Combe but Lank Combe, roughly a half mile to the north.[2] The romance gave a local habitation to shadowy figures of West Country history and legend; and the great moor, wonderful in itself, took on the aura of a mythic landscape. The process was under way by 1871 when Arthur Munby noted that *Lorna Doone* "has had. . .the effect of arousing among people on the spot a keen interest in their own legends."[3] For pilgrims to Doone-land, the heroine, the outlaws, and the stalwart farmer are still presences on Exmoor, much as Tess or Diggory Venn are in Hardy's Wessex. All the concern with finding the true Doone Valley, the waterslide, and the site of Plover's Barrows is a sign of the characters' life within the imagination. They are the spirits of a place, and the mind seeks the place that matches their reality.

But their appeal is wider than Devon and Somerset and deeper than Exmoor history and legend. Lorna, John Ridd, and the outlaw Carver Doone live in the imagination because they are caught in a struggle of large mythic dimensions. The struggle has the shape of a seasonal myth in which Lorna—like earlier flower-maidens in

49

Blackmore—reflects the life of springtime. As Northrop Frye has
pointed out, her role is like Persephone's in the Greek myth of death
and renewal.[4] Abducted as a child at the end of autumn, when the
story begins, she grows up under the threat of Carver Doone, who
tries to force her to marry him during the Great Winter. Her champion is the narrator, John Ridd, whose father was killed by the
Doones just before the girl was captured and made an orphan. As a
boy on a farm with his mother and two sisters, he discovers the captive princess of a "realm of violence," and he returns to the valley
as a man ready to love her and to become a protector of life against
the deadly brutality of the Doones. But to win the heroine, he must
also confront his own potential for brutality during an initiation that
brings him, at its worst, to a sense of complete loss. Like the hero of
Cradock Nowell, John is born for trial. His part is to "learn by feeling (whereby alone we can learn) that all the clefts of anguish, and
the rifts into the heart of us" are "but the needful entrance for the
grafts of fruit eternal."[5]

Lorna's abduction, captivity, and eventual return provide a
natural pattern for a story of initiation, since the most famous and
obscure of ancient initiatory rites concerned the abduction and
return of Persephone. She was a focal deity in the Mysteries honor-
ing her and her mother, the grain-goddess Demeter, at Athens and
Eleusis, where parts of her story may have been reenacted.[6] In *Lorna Doone*, the significance of John's ordeals can be seen in terms of
an analogy with the ancient myth and initiation. Like Hercules,
who supposedly sought to be purified in the Lesser Mysteries at
Athens before battling the powers of the underworld, John has to be
purged of fear and his own violent impulses as he confronts the
Doones. His ordeals bring him to the verge of death in spirit and
body after Carver shoots down his bride at the altar. But his initiation follows the seasonal cycle, beginning with winter and ending
providentially with summer. Lorna returns, like the lost Persephone
in the Mysteries, in a scene comparable to the return of Hermione
in *The Winter's Tale* or the sudden recovery of the bride after the
last shot in Weber's opera *Der Freischütz* (1821). The experience
leaves John with a sense of blessedness and confidence such as
Cicero gained at Eleusis: "We have been given a reason not only to
live in joy but also to die with a better hope."[7] Both the romance
and the ancient rite challenge the mind to conceive of new life
springing from apparent death; both supply some of "the symbols
that carry human spirit forward."[8] The vision of his bride's return

gives John his basic reason for telling the story, for it is still a source of joy and hope for him as an ageing man, nearing the time of his own death.

The fresh viewpoint of the initiated narrator is part of his story's appeal. John's quickened sense of life informs everything he describes—all that grows, moves, changes under the influence of the seasons. For one early reviewer, the effect was like being transported from London to breathe the "pure air" of the country.[9] Thomas Hardy wrote Blackmore in 1875 to say "how astonished I was to find" that *Lorna Doone* contained "exquisite ways of describing things which are more after my own heart than the 'presentations' of any other writer I am acquainted with. . . . Little phases of nature which I thought nobody had noticed but myself were continually turning up in your book—for instance, the marking of a heap of sand into little pits by the droppings from trees was a fact I should unhesitatingly have declared unknown to any other novelist till now."[10] He was referring to the account of crossing Exmoor in the fog, when John and his servant John Fry ride home from Blundell's School, passing "little stubby trees that. . .were drizzled with a mass of wet, and hung their points with dropping." The passage shows the keenness of John's perception as he re-creates a scene from boyhood and reveals the child's anxious need to stay in touch with the physical world:

Wherever the butt-end of a hedgerow came up from the hollow ground, like the withers of a horse, holes of splash were pocked and pimpled in the yellow sand of coneys, or under the dwarf tree's ovens. But soon it was too dark to see that, or anything else, I may say, except the creases in the dusk, where prisoned light crept up the valleys.

And after a while even that was gone, and no other comfort left to us, except to see our horses' heads jogging to their footsteps, and the dark ground pass below us, lighter where the wet was; and then the splash, foot after foot, more clever than we can do it, and the orderly jerk of the tail, and the smell of what a horse is. (ch. III)

The rhythms of a flowing syntax as well as the images evoke the feelings of their dark progress, showing why Wilfred Meynell praised Blackmore's ability not only to enter the "large and single soul of his hero," but to "feel from within" the lives "of a horse and of a dog and of a vine putting forth tendrils."[11] John's attention to the distinctiveness of things ("the smell of what a horse is") fills his narrative with what Gerard Manley Hopkins might have termed "inscapes" of West Country life. The poet admired Blackmore's "great strokes" of description, which sometimes have a hint of Hopkins as well as a "really Shakespearean" ring. [12] Hopkins's storm in "The Wreck of the Deutschland" (1876), with its "wiry and white-fiery and whirlwind-swivellèd snow," is foreshadowed by the less stunning but still brilliant prose account of the Great Winter, when John found a huge drift "rolling and curling beneath the violent blast, tufting and combing with rustling swirls. . .while from the smothering sky, more and more fiercely at every blast, came the pelting pitiless arrows, winged with murky white, and pointed with the barbs of frost" (ch. 42). In *Lorna Doone* as well as in "The Wreck of the Deutschland," nature's violence is accepted as a dark manifestation of providence, not as a sign of cosmic uncaring or malice. [13] "God shapes all our fitness, and gives each man his meaning," John writes, "even as he guides the wavering lines of snow descending" (ch. 42). His sense of divine activity in the world is one sign of the sacramental vision shared by Hopkins and Meynell, both Roman Catholics, and the Anglican Blackmore. John can perceive "the grandeur of God" in nature; and, in a passage which Meynell praised, he responds with Hopkins's spirit to the return of dawn: "life and joy sprang reassured from every crouching hollow; every flower, and bud, and bird, had a fluttering sense of them; and all the flashing of God's gaze merged into soft beneficence" (ch. 33).

John's lively perception of the world is one of several gifts that make him a rarity of Victorian fiction—a "genuine" hero. [14] Not only evoking the distinctive realities of plants, animals, and other people, he also expresses his own highly "selved" uniqueness as a man of humor and prejudice, sympathy and egotism and full awareness of the force of life within his body. His vitality is so strong that the reader feels it almost as his own. [15] The flow of energy through his narrative has touched such diverse people as the Victorian curate and diarist Francis Kilvert, who heard his father read "that wild and powerful book" aloud to the family in 1872, [16] and the adolescent D. H. Lawrence and Jessie Chambers (the Miriam of *Sons and Lovers*), who transplanted Bagworthy Forest to Nottingham and "scoured down the hillside with imaginary Doones at [their] heels." [17] A twenty-year-old artist dying of tuberculosis continued until a very few days of his death to read and reread the "spirit-stirring story." His father, the Pre-Raphaelite painter Ford Madox Brown, reported his love for the book as a tribute to the author's "powers of fascinating" his readers.[18] But the powers are immediately those of his greatest persona, the narrator who both conveys and is himself an expression of Blackmore's gusto in depicting fully developed creatures, from a trout with "shoulders vast; the spring of [whose] back was like a rainbow,"[19] to the mighty rustic wrestlers (akin to Hopkins's Harry Ploughman and Felix Randal) in *Clara Vaughan* and *Perlycross*. From the moment that John defeats Robin Snell at Blundell's School, he offers vicarious fulfillment of any man's or boy's dreams of physical achievement. Certainly he more than compensates for the limitations of his creator, who as a "small, unhealthy-looking boy" at the same school took the loser's role in such battles.[20]

But the opening battle in the schoolyard introduces a conflict of values which John never quite resolves and which recurs in Blackmore's fiction. It arises from the impulse to celebrate and to rely upon physical force, despite the voice of a Christian conscience. As a child already victorious in some sixty battles, John hesitates before yielding to the heroic code of honor and the tooth-for-a-tooth morality of the schoolboys. But John Fry's advice proves decisive: "Chraist's will be done; I zim thee had better faight, Jan". John fights, and he grows up to kill in meeting force with force in the final raid upon the Doone Valley. Warfare makes his story a "prose epic," as Sir Herbert Warren called it,[21] with the pastoral and romantic themes set within an epical movement toward a showdown with the enemy. Naturally the hero must play a key role in driving the outlaws from their stronghold. But the violence of the community's revenge causes him to doubt the rightness of it in his "latter years" when he considers the judgment of God, "the front of whose forehead is mercy" (ch. 71).

John's developing conscience is historically important for he appeared in fiction at a time when the impulse to idolize strength was pervasive in the Victorian novel.[22] In Charles Kingsley's *Westward Ho!* (1855), an earlier romantic epic of North Devon, the author condones violence as long as it expresses national rather than merely personal revenge. The huge blond hero, Amyas Leigh, speaks coolly of cutting off a Frenchman's head, and Kingsley apparently approves the act as an honorable way for a young Elizabethan gentleman to flesh his "maiden sword": the Frenchman, after all, had spoken slanderously against the queen.[23] The narrator of *Lorna Doone* is less confident in rationalizing violence. At the same time, his usual kindness and self-control set him squarely against a rising type of Victorian antihero—the "muscular libertine," cynical, "tall, strong, black-browed, and terrible, as Saul," in George Lawrence's *Guy Livingstone* (1857).[24] In Carver Doone, John confronts a crude emblem of irresponsible masculine power, which in more sophisticated figures became an attraction in popular late-Victorian fiction.[25]

John has conscience without the self-conscious virtues of the Muscular Christian, and he has power without the irresponsibility of the muscular libertine. For anyone who wished to believe with G. K. Chesterton that "the mighty are merciful,"[26] he could offer comforting reassurance. But his might has to be tested, disciplined, and at one point broken as he grows in the virtues which Blackmore eventually ranked above strength and heroism: "patience, cheerfulness, and modesty, truth, simplicity, and loving-kindness."[27] Judged by these values, John falls short of longer-suffering men in Blackmore's later work— of "Captain Larks" in *Christowell* and the Rev. Penniloe in *Perlycross*. But he can be known far more intimately than these characters, and by recreating his experience he lets the reader feel the impulse toward violence while moving toward a fuller sense of the need for patience, mercy, and self-control.

His inner life is revealed through analogies with the visible world. A tree frozen in the terrible winter reflects his sense of how outward losses accompany development from within: "Our great walnut lost three branches, and has been dying ever since: though growing meanwhile, as the soul does" (ch. 42). Like those of plants, the positive movements of his initiation are upward and toward the light. His climb up the waterslide as a fourteen-year-old boy brings the threat of drowning in a pool of black water, but it ends with brightness and fresh air about him, a loss of consciousness, an awakening to find the child Lorna kneeling beside him, and by her "(like an early star). . .the first primrose of the season" (ch. 8). The boy offers her a gift of fish; on his return seven years later, he brings her eggs, and with this gift he enters her bower, the symbolic goal of all his questing. By describing the freshness of this place, he expresses the appeal of Lorna's womanhood. His accounts of coming to meet her there reflect his sexual feeling and are in this way comparable to the story of Leander swimming at night to Hero, which Blackmore had translated from Musaeus. His journeys up the valley form the springtime movement of his initiation, when "bowering newness tempts us ever forward." "We rise into quick sense of life, and spring through clouds of mystery" (ch. 19).

Wintry forces oppose this movement, shadowing his story with the dark side of vegetation myths: the end of the growing season, the death of the corn-spirit and the descent of Persephone to the underworld. That myth is never fully realized in the romance, because another motif—the rescue of the captive maiden—makes the heroine as much like Andromeda as Persephone. An attractive subject in Victorian poetry, the bride of Perseus had appeared in a narrative poem by Charles Kingsley and would appear again in a sonnet by Hopkins; Browning alludes to her in *The Ring and the Book*, which was published in the same year as *Lorna Doone*. The story of Alcestis may also be in the background of the romance, for Lorna has a Herculean champion who tries to wrest her from a deathly power.[28] But hers are the attributes of a floral goddess who disappears at the start of winter and returns to the story in the spring. Her enemy is Carver Doone, the dark force analogous to the Lord of the Dead who abducts Persephone. Black-bearded and armed always with a gun, Carver almost matches the hero in strength while surpassing most villains of Victorian melodrama in deeds of murder and rape and in the number of his wives. He illustrates what John means by speaking of man's "instinct" of death, "which accounts for his slaying his fellow men so, and every other creature" (ch. 41). Carver's power darkens Lorna's spirit, convincing her that escape and happiness are imposssible: " 'It can never, never be,' she murmured to herself alone: 'Who am I, to dream of it' "(ch. 33).

At such moments, she has the pensiveness, without the sultriness, of the goddess holding the pomegranate in Rossetti's painting. Her name begins with a suggestion of forlornnness and ends with an echo of "doom" (her song in chapter 16 of the first edition closed with "the doom of death"). The sound of her old name in later years brings back "forgotten sadness" (ch. 75). Her thralldom to Carver's power persists even after John rescues her from the snow-bound valley. Carver violates the spring at Plover's Barrows by appearing suddenly before her with his gun and firing between her feet, and then demands that she come back to him the next day. Fearing an attack upon the Ridds, Lorna begs John to let her go; had he not been resolute, she would have reenacted Persephone's return to her dark lord.

John's initiation is to confront the extremes of spring and winter, tenderness and cruelty, embodied in Lorna and Carver. To become her worthy champion in the conflict, he must be cleansed of the violence that is potential in himself and fully realized in the villain. By disposition he is on the side of life. He has the vitality of a tremendous natural force: he fishes, he swims flooding rivers, he plays and wrestles with "fiercest cattle" (ch. 29). He feels his brotherhood with the animals, picturing himself as a "sacrificial bull" (ch. 56), a sheep, a feeding pig. As a farmer, he fosters and protects life, rescuing sheep from the snowdrift and leading the reapers down the field at harvest. He works in active alliance with the "dumb-loving motherhood" of nature that seems to surround him.[29] Of all the characters, John is closest to this sense of the natural world which Demeter, the mother of Persephone, embodied in Greek mythology. Not even Mrs. Ridd has quite the homely grandeur of an earth-mother, but John conveys some feeling of Demeter's persence when he tells how her emblem, a "neck of corn, dressed with ribbons gaily" (ch. 29), is lifted up and honored as fervently, if not as reverently, as it was at Eleusis, where a sheaf of wheat was a key symbol of rebirth. John's account of the rustic bellowing of the Exmoor harvest-song, and of the earlier blessing of the harvest, recalls the festivities commanded by Virgil in Blackmore's translation of the first Georgic:

> Let all your farm lads bow at Ceres' shrine,
> And mix her cakes with honey, milk, and wine;
> Thrice round the crops the goodly victim bear,
> While all the choir and merry neighbours share,
> And Ceres' visit with a shout invoke;
>   Let no man lay a sickle to the grain
> Or ere in Ceres' honour, crowned with oak,
>   He foot the unstudied dance and chant the strain. (11.395ff.)

For readers who recall Theocritus as well as Virgil, John further suggests the presence of a harvest-spirit when he tells of seeing a vision of his love in the "whirling yellow world" of falling wheat stalks and then of daydreaming like the love-sick reaper in Idyll X, which ends with a song to Demeter.[30] Though he lacks a name for her, he knows something of what Demeter represents; and with the shooting of Lorna, he will learn what she experienced: the emotion of wasting loss. [31]

With all his protective exploits, the young farmer earns the comparison with Hercules which James II makes before knighting him (ch. 68). He will cleanse Exmoor of the outlaws, and already in tending the wounds of Tom Faggus and Ruth Huckaback he has shown something of the healing powers that were ascribed to the ancient hero. But his final ordeal will call for more than physical vitality. To keep from using his strength as rashly as Hercules or as cruelly as his antagonist, he must overcome the "evil spirit" that heats his blood and sets his muscles "tingling for a mighty throw" (ch. 36). Since boyhood when he said, "This for my father's murderer" as he practiced shooting, he has been in danger of warping his life with a passion for revenge (ch. 6). He outgrows the urge more easily than Clara Vaughan in Blackmore's first novel, but violence always attracts him. Even as an elderly narrator, he refuses to dwell upon a scene of fighting because it "breeds such savage delight in me" (ch. 72). Like a character in Blackmore's later fiction, he could have said, "The enemy I feared, in the burst of pent-up fury, was myself."[32]

One unacted impulse and two outbursts are enough to show his potential brutality. The first is a merely comic longing to throw the highwayman Tom Faggus and his famous horse over the farmyard gate: Tom has proposed to Anne Ridd, and John wants her affections and excellent cooking all to himself. He does not want a reformed criminal for a brother-in-law, despite his eagerness to marry a girl raised by the Doones. When his violence really bursts out, there is irony with no humor. After his horse bites Ruth Huckaback, he nearly breaks the animal's jaw: a man can be "more vicious" than any horse, he comments, without mentioning his own cruelty to Ruth by first flirting with her and then inviting her to his wedding. He erupts again after his capture in Monmouth's Rebellion, when he is roped, mocked, and threatened with hanging from a "fatal tree" already burdened with two dead men. Thoroughly frightened, John acts neither as a martyr nor as a stoic hero, and when a soldier tries to spit in his face he strikes back with a killing blow. He is still the natural man, acting with brute strength and "pride" (ch. 65). His essential healthfulness is suggested soon afterwards by the symbols of life on his brand-new coat of arms: the wheat-sheaf upon a field of green, the three red cakes for nourishment and the red for his ruddiness—"Ridd" being a form of "red."[33] But the other emblems—the black raven, the lion, and the two-headed boar—do more than create a little comedy of heraldic extravagance. They indicate dangers to be overcome within himself as well as in the world about him, and they suggest his need to be purified, like Hercules, the sometimes monstrous slayer of monsters.

John's pent-up violence is tested in every encounter with Carver Doone. Carver represents all that the young man fears from within and from without. His changing attitude toward the villain marks the stages of his development. In early manhood he moves from terror to a moment of longing for the outlaw's cunning and "relish for blood," a wish which he quickly rejects (ch. 38). Then his fear lessens as the desire grows to master his rival in physical combat. This urge to prove himself against the human image of his fear partially accounts for his refusal to shoot when Carver comes at night to ravage Plover's Barrows. The narrator still puzzles over his failure to pull the trigger: "Would to God that I had done so!" (ch. 49). Instead, he insults the villain and throws him into the barnyard muck. This "straightforward" triumph at once gratifies his ego and shields his conscience from the guilt of murder.

At the same time, the refusal to shoot may reflect a dim awareness of his kinship with "that vile Carver," for whom he was once mistaken at night in the Doone Valley (ch. 37). If in this romance Carver has the role of a double, embodying the repressed impulses of the hero, then for John to kill him would be in symbolic terms a partial act of self-destruction. As François Lenormant pointed out in 1864, the hero and the monster he combats may each represent an aspect of the same being.[34] Ancient myths treat the monster's death as the hero's triumph, but in a nineteenth-century romance, such as *Dr. Jekyll and Mr. Hyde*, seeking to kill the double can be suicidal. (The narrator of Conrad's "Secret Sharer" gains maturity by letting his double go free.) A warning of the danger comes to John in the final attack on the Doone Valley. There an enraged farmer finds the outlaw who had taken his wife; somehow, "without weapon," each man kills the other (ch. 71). Soon afterwards, John and Carver fight in a weaponless struggle which almost ends with the death of both men in the Wizard's Slough, the "grave of slime" left for a soul destroyed by its own selfishness.

Carver's shooting of the bride at the altar is the strangest sign of his symbolic role. After wishing to put a bullet through John's brain (ch. 38), why does he aim at Lorna instead? He gives no answer except to say that he was punishing John for his "impertinence" (ch. 74). His action makes clearer sense in terms of the conflict between life-giving and destructive forces. To kill the bride, the embodiment of fresh life, is the death-lord's surest way of possessing her. From the viewpoint of Jungian psychology, the act might appear as a movement of the unconscious to resist integration with the rest of the psyche. In myth, wholeness is signified by the union of the hero and the rescued maiden. She is the anima, freed from the distorting fears that keep the feminine image of the soul locked in unconsciousness.[35] In striking out against her, Carver vents the destructiveness of a one-sided, trigger-happy masculinity, bent on self-assertion and unwilling to love. To destroy the bride is to deny the wholeness that marriage expresses and the place of a woman in a mutual relationship with a man. The crime stuns the hero, reducing him at last to an instrument of vengeance, the very thing that Carver has become.

But in their struggle at the Wizard's Slough, he does not persist in his resolve to kill. Painfully wounded for the first time in the story, John withstands the force of the outlaw's clench, chokes the strength from him, exhausts his fury, and offers Carver freedom. At this moment, both men are almost lost in the slime. John leaps back, while Carver sinks like Grendel, his arm unstrung from the hero's grasp, into the slough. Insofar as he plays a symbolic role, he should vanish at this point. By offering him freedom, John outgrows the potential for brutality that his double has enacted. At the moment of his triumph, the hero sees the lost man in Carver, and the monster that he feared and hated sinks from sight.

With the shooting of Lorna comes the darkest phase of his initiation, the time comparable to the mourning for the lost Persephone at Eleusis. He has no faith in the report that she still lives, and her image gives way to "the black cauldron of the wizard's death" that boils within his brain (ch. 75). He grows passive, losing "conceit of strength" in his sickness and enduring "fires of pain" with no more fear of dying. Ahead he can see only an image of the "black and worthless burden of life" that hangs in his mind "like the bead in a wisp of frog-spawn." His sense of arrested development— the "tadpole life" without Lorna—marks Carver's apparent success in blocking spiritual growth.

But initiatory death is the way of rebirth. John's weakness and the image of frog-spawn mark the reduction of his being to its beginnings, so that the self can be re-formed. Signs of renewal have appeared, already, even at the final battleground. After Carver vanishes, his child comes back to John carrying bluebells, the wild hyacinths that are emblems of resurrection. The boy keeps alive the hero's waning kindness. John must ride home with the dead man's son in his arms, holding a living proof that good can issue from evil, for Carver has fathered a "loving child." A second hopeful sign is the coming of Ruth as the healer for John and Lorna. Like Paulina in *The Winter's Tale*, she presides over the mysteries of rebirth. She has earned this role by suffering wounds of her own and by resisting the temptation of bitterness and jealousy; her name means the compassion that overcomes vengeance. Ruth has kept faith where the hero wavered: she refused to doubt that Lorna would marry him, or to accept the doctor's word that she was dead. Ruth's hands remove the bullet from Lorna's side, and her resolve saves John from being bled to death by his physicians. Decked with flowers like a celebrant in a midsummer ceremony, she is the one who leads the bride to her husband for their surprising reunion.

This scene may be too great a challenge to poetic faith, especially for readers who prefer the conventions of the realistic novel. But a happy ending has been prepared for, if only by John's gusto in telling the story. The ending also completes the initiatory theme and the symbolic patterns that are traditional in romance. Marriage signifies and promises renewal, and its symbolic value in *Lorna Doone* is shown by the transference of dominant colors in the last episode. John's redness is given to the heroine, whose blood stains her white bridal gown and his vest at the altar. After many. bleedings, he takes her former color, looking at his weakened hands and thinking that "Lorna's could scarcely have been whiter." At their reunion, she is the active one, rushing to his arms, free from her role as the passive captive. John has learned passivity and dependence on others' care while being cleansed through suffering. His whiteness marks his purification, and the sharing of their colors signifies renewal through the joining of lives in marriage. According to Northrop Frye, the red and white on St. George's shield in Book I of *The Faerie Queene* are emblematic of both sexual union and the resurrection; as an analogue, Frye points to alchemy, where "a crucial phase of the production of the elixir of immortality is known as the union of the red king and the white queen."[36] Alchemy may have had nothing to do with Blackmore's imagery (though an astrologer-alchemist appears later in *Alice Lorraine*); still, the special values of red and white belong to his romance of initiatory death and rebirth.

For the hero, the bride's return brings a sense of new life that is both sexual and spiritual. In the first edition, there was more stress upon sexual renewal: "'I felt my life come back, and warm; I felt my trust in woman flow; I felt the joy of living now, and the power of doing it." Blackmore revised the passage to express further dimensions of John's experience: "I felt my life come back, and glow; I felt my trust in God revive; I felt the joy of living and of loving dearer things than life." Like an initiate in the Mysteries, he has been given "a reason not only to live in joy but also to die with a better hope."[37] Lorna's return offers him a vision of felicity, a glimpse of the "lost paradise" barely to be dreamed of in a world of violence and fear.[38]

For the hero to realize this vision may seem as fantastic as a fairy tale, but nothing less than the union of a man and a woman conveys the wholeness of his rebirth.[39] Their marriage also completes the analogy with one nineteenth-century view of the symbolism of the Eleusinian Mysteries. According to François Lenormant, the soul's entry into a state of blessedness was "habitually represented as a scene of love, " with at least two Greek vases showing "the marriage of the initiated young man with Eudaimonia [Felicity]. The corresponding mythological expression is that which makes the dead man the husband of Persephone. . . ."[40] Lorna brings John a sense of blessedness in this life, and through her return he feels the promise of blessedness in the life to come. Their marriage affirms the power of love and celebrates the soul's movement toward felicity and light. The reader who feels pleasure at their union takes part in the celebration.

CHAPTER 4

The Perils of Success: Novels of the 1870s

How many chances have I missed! How many times might I have advanced to stern respectability.[1]

WITH the publication of *Lorna Doone* in three volumes in April 1869, Blackmore finally came into his own as a novelist. But in spite of an encouraging review in the *Athenaeum*,[2] the public showed little awareness of his achievement until late in 1870, after the book reappeared in a cheap one-volume edition and Queen Victoria approved the engagement of Princess Louise to a Scottish nobleman, the marquis of Lorne. With the heroine being a descendant of the lords of Lorne, the literary romance was swept into the royal one, and by the year's end Blackmore noted the "great rush upon Lorna; what a hap-hazard lot the public are."[3] Because of their fickleness, he was able to begin bargaining for the serialization of this next book in the prestigious *Blackwood's Magazine*. John Blackwood, the publisher of such current favorites as George Eliot and Bulwer-Lytton, hesitated while reading the first two installments of *The Maid of Sker* in the author's tiny handwriting—"Flea-like," as Blackmore confessed (27 February 1871). But by March of 1871 Blackwood's mind was made up: he would admit the author of *Lorna Doone* into the highest circle of British novelists.

This apparent triumph turned out to be a source of frustration for Blackmore throughout most of the decade. *Lorna Doone* had given him enough fame to do an aesthetically and psychologically hazardous thing. He could now sell a virtually unwritten novel and then race to finish it while the chapters appeared in regular monthly installments. Blackwood accepted *The Maid of Sker* after seeing only the first installments; not more than four of the eventual twelve were completed when the first one appeared in August 1871. Contrary to the rumors that Blackmore wrote the first draft of this book in his school days, his letters show that the story was far from finished, and that he was trying rather desperately to keep ahead of the printer. Orchard work, fights among his field hands, visits from his beloved niece Eva Pinto-Leite, and an attack of epilepsy all complicated the task of completing the novel on schedule. When the narrator in the first chapter says, "Thus I begin, but never end, the tale I now begin to you, and perhaps shall never end it" (3), he apparently speaks for the author as well. One installment might be lively, but did he know where the story was headed? When John Blackwood delicately asked what the total "fabric" of the novel would be like,[4] Blackmore only answered with a short-sighted rationalization: "To me it appears to matter little, for the uses of a magazine, whether a tale be perfect in plot, construction, & so on—in other words *as a whole*—so long as it is truly written, interesting, and amusing" (27 February 1871). He ignored the obvious: a serial eventually would be read and judged in book form, and any great novel would have to be more than the sum of its monthly parts.

Blackmore knew these facts in some corner of his mind, for he had admitted long ago that "real success" in fiction depended upon fashioning a "closely-knitted plot."[5] He could offer sound critical advice to his friend, the poet and novelist Mortimer Collins: "You never seem to me to take a character, & work it out; but to conceive a whole lot, & let them go to the devil afterwards. Improbabilities are nothing; of them I take small heed, but I can't help knowg. when a man cares for his work, & when he doesn't. Page after page ought to be cut out, & for God's sake try not to be clever [wh. you need not *try* for] but to be a little natural. Try to be dull, my dear fellow, & give us no more epigrams."[6]

Though his remark about improbabilities would have shocked George Eliot or Henry James, the letter expresses real concern with the craft of fiction. Unlike the free-and-easy Collins, Blackmore cared deeply for his work, whether he was pruning a tree or revising a manuscript. But the two tasks kept interfering with each other, while the need to please a distinguished publisher and to keep ahead of the printer made composition a frustrating chore. Repeatedly he failed to give fiction a satisfying form in this decade, and he knew it.

I   *The Alien Sensibility in* The Maid of Sker

The material to be shaped into fictional form in *The Maid of Sker* came primarily from Blackmore's boyhood visits to Newton Nottage in Glamorganshire. From the Blackmores he had learned about Exmoor, and from his mother's family he came to know the history and the sandy coastal landscape of this neighborhood in Wales. His uncle, the Rev. Henry Hey Knight, was a scholarly antiquarian who published an "Account of Newton Nottage" in the *Archaeologia Cambrensis* (1853), cited early in the novel (72). According to the author's letter to Blackwood, the title came from an "ancient ballad" (31 [Dec.] 1870). Though the legend told in the ballad, "The Maid of Sker," bears little relation to the plot of the novel, the gloomy Sker House, just west of Portcawl in the sand dunes, is a central image for Blackmore. And the purported author of the ballad, "David Llewellyn, a bard of Newton Nottage,"[7] has the same name as the narrator, a character of bardic claims who may have been drawn from a Welshman known to Blackmore in boyhood.

Other materials came from beyond Wales. The nominal heroine, the lost child "Bardie," is drawn from Blackmore's precocious niece whom he called by that name and described in doting letters to his publisher: "She knows all the operas now, & performs the shadow-dance & several of the dying scenes. She was only 3 years old, when she uttered that magnificent satire upon the ladies of the age—'I'll go to the opeya in a low-necked dress, & show all my stomach, with a necklace over it!' " (4 July 1871). Not content with transcribing her baby-talk for Blackwood, he put some of it into the novel: to his ears, if to no one else's, it was the language of the muse: "If anything happened to her, I never could lay pen again to the Maid of Sker." An opposite source of inspiration supplied the villain, the demonic Parson Chowne, a recognizable portrait of the Rev. John Froude, notorious in Devon in the early nineteenth century. Blackmore's father called him a "shocking fellow—a disgrace to the Church. The less we say about him the better." But his fame had already spread to Edinburgh, where John Blackwood described his scandalous treatment of a bishop in an anecdote which found its way into the novel.[8] Chowne's brawling companion, the Rev. Jack Rambone, a boxer and wrestler, was drawn from the sporting parson Jack Radford, who "went with a scissors-grinding truck all over Wales and Cornwall, challenging all comers to fist or fore-hip."[9] To make these clergymen "seem less impossible," Blackmore put them back "50 years"[10] before their time in a novel covering the period between 1782 and the close of the century.

So long a time-span spelled problems for organizing a coherent story. Lacking a strong plot, the book wavers between reporting the picaresque adventures of the narrator and unfolding the romance of the abandoned child who grows up among Welsh fishing-folk before rejoining her noble family. The child is too young to play a central role when David Llewellyn finds her, and David himself, "a most repulsive old vagabound," according to one reviewer,[11] is not a fascinating candidate for a picaresque hero. But the discovery changes his life, and in showing the rogue's response to the child Blackmore begins to create a story.

David is caught from the first in a conflict of motives. Trying to provide a home for his own granddaughter and Bardie, he schemes dishonestly to keep possession of the boat that brought the child ashore. When his fishing business fails, he gets caught in a more dangerous conflict. Moving across the Bristol Channel to Braunton Burrows in North Devon, he becomes a spy for Parson Chowne, the demon who gains at least temporary possession of his soul. But his allegiances shift to the young couple whom Chowne wants to destroy. Suspecting treachery, Chowne tries to burn his henchman alive in his boat, but David retaliates by firing the parson's fourteen ricks of wheat, afterwards reporting his exploit in a style that particularly gratifies the beautiful Miss Carey, Chowne's intended victim:

"You dear old Davy," she said, "I never thought you had so much courage. You are the very bravest man—but stop, did you burn the whole of them?"

"Every one burned itself, your ladyship; I saw the ashes dying down, and his summer-house as well took fire, through the mischief of the wind, and all his winter stock of wood, and his tool-house, and his—"

"Any more, any more, old David?"

"Yes, your ladyship, his cow-house, after the cows were all set free, and his new cart-shed fifty feet long, also his carpenter's shop, and his cider-press."

"You are the very best man," she answered, with her beautiful eyes full upon me, "that I have seen, since I was a child. I must think what to do for you. Did you burn anything more, old Davy?"

"The fire did, your ladyship, three large barns, and a thing they call a 'linhay'; also the granary, and the meal-house, and the apple-room, and the

churn-room, and only missed the dairy by a little nasty slant of wind."
(264 - 65)

Finely drawn out to win the largest possible reward from Miss
Carey, David's report is one of the last highlights in a story that
begins to falter once he rejoins the Royal Navy to escape Parson
Chowne, "for whom the French fleet proves a poor substitute."[12]
Only if the novel is read as a dramatic monologue, constantly
revealing the narrator's shifty character, can it be enjoyed to the
end. Inspired by Defoe's rogue-narrators, "Old Dyo" is the most
complex persona that Blackmore ever created.[13] He suggests the influence of Browning, though Blackmore's opinion of the poet who
made him doubt his own sanity has already been cited. A mixture of
sentimentality and worldliness, the salty fisherman dotes upon the
infant heroine, yet consoles a man whose shrewish wife is in her
seventh pregnancy by recollecting "more than twenty instances of
excellent women who had managed six, and gone off at the seventh
visitation" (309). He is a trickster, expert at selling rotten fish after
propping outward their sunken eyes with spines placed inside the
mouth, and he is fascinated by all stories of successful deceit and
retaliation. This fascination gives him a certain kinship with the
sewing-machine salesman who narrates William Faulkner's Snopes
trilogy. David's story of barn-burning has its parallels in Faulkner,
and so does his account of the viciousness of a frustrated horse-
trader. When Parson Chowne fails to get a gentleman's fine mount,
he slips the poisonous red seeds of the "Stinking Iris" inside the
horse's eyelids; on the ride home, the animal goes mad from the
berries "heating and melting" and "shooting their red fire over the
agonized tissues of eyeballs" (173). The owner is found half dead
and the horse is sent to the knacker.

Fascinated by cunning, brutality, and pain, David has a
Faulknerian eye for the grotesque. This comes out repeatedly in his
narrative, whether he is describing a man dying of rabies or the
crooked-legged naked people on the dunes of Nympton Moor or the
crooked-minded hypocrisy of his Methodist neighbor in Wales,
Hezikiah Perkins, or of the old woman in the crowd of eager
salvagers on the beach where a slave-ship is breaking up: "the Lord
may bless my poor endeavours to rescue them poor Injuns. But I
can't get on without a rake" (66). Yet David can create a sense of
tragic irony when he tells how a drunken father, suspecting no
danger, sees the "carcasses" of his five strong sons uncovered from

the sand. Then he launches into a boastful account of selling stale fish to his neighbors. His way of reporting life is almost as grotesque as what he sees. It is part of his role as a Welsh antihero, almost totally opposite to the honest Saxon John Ridd.[14] His viewpoint reflects the alien sensibility of a man who confesses his failure to attain the "stern respectability" of Victorian England.

Perhaps as a warning to erudite readers, Blackmore prefaced the novel with a Greek epigraph from Theognis: "Away with you, hateful to gods, and faithless to men, *you* who had in your bosom a chilly spotted snake."[15] The line could apply to Chowne, but David too is treasonous, and the villainy of the one is the roguery of the other written in Satanic letters across the sky. For this reason, the epigraph can be taken also as a signal to keep a safe distance from the narrator. David at first distressed John Blackwood, who questioned the wisdom of writing a whole novel from a rogue's point of view. After doubting that the Welshman would be "sufficiently attractive and entertaining," Blackwood read far enough to declare him "a wonderful fellow . . . capitally sustained."[16] But reviewers had graver doubts, with the *Examiner* calling it a "mistake" to write from the viewpoint of a "vulgar, cunning, selfish," and in the worst sense "sophisticated" fisherman, who keeps the story "on a low plane of thought and sentiment."[17] Even after Blackmore bowdlerized his version of eighteenth-century life to suit a "far more deeply wicked age of delicate hypocrisy" (16 January 1872), David's style remained salty. What properly Victorian narrator would refer to a sailor's daughter as "his only child that we knew of" (3 - 4) or tell of flirting with a married former sweetheart just a few days after his wife's funeral? The critic in the *Examiner* wondered how any respectable reader could bear to "keep company with him through three whole volumes."

What makes this low outsider particularly distressing is the way he mingles his roguish attitudes with some well-known Victorian ones. Taffy was a Welshman and therefore a thief in English eyes, but this Taffy rivals the best Victorian Englishman in patriotism, jingoism, racism, worship of little girls, and keen sensitivity to nature. He describes the life of the seashore with Ruskin's passion for accuracy just as Hopkins, Kilvert, and scores of less talented Englishmen were doing at the time when Blackmore was writing. At low tide, David notes how "the bladder weeds hang trickling, and the limpets close their valves, and the beautiful jelly-flowers look no better than chilblains," and then gives a contrasting picture of a tidal pool "alive with birds." Wild ducks charm him, "arching their necks, and preening themselves, titivating (as we call it) with their bills in and out the down, and shoulders up to run the wet off; then turning their heads, as if on a swivel, they fettle their backs and their scapular plume. Then . . . they begin to think of their dinners, and with stretched necks down they dive to catch some luscious morsel, and all you can see is a little sharp tail and a pair of red feet kicking" (10). But the next sentence breaks the illusion that David is a disciple of Ruskin: "Bless all their innocent souls, how often I longed to have a good shot at them, and might have killed eight or ten at a time with a long gun heavily loaded!"

A harsher discord with proper Victorian tones comes into his account of a sinking slave-ship—a subject treated with famous eloquence by Ruskin in volume one of *Modern Painters*. David touches the storm clouds with Ruskin and Turner's brush as he tells how the "upper heaven" was all a "spread of burning yellow," the "half-way sky . . . red as blood with fibres under it," and the whole "whirling, tossing upward jets of darkness" (39). But he lacks Ruskin's humanitarian tone. David does call the drowning slaves "poor things," but he assures his readers that he is not "such a fool as to dream . . . that a negro is 'our own flesh and blood, and a brother immortal,' as the parsons begin to prate, under some dark infection. They differ from us a great deal more than an ass does from a horse; but for all that I was right down glad—as a man of loving-kindness—that such a pelt of rain came up as saved me from the discomfort—or pain, if you must have the truth—of beholding several score, no doubt, of unfortunate blacks a-drowning" (47).

His tone is complexly offensive. Doctrinaire racism, with an ugly word-play on "dark infection," meets an opposite current of humane sympathy, of which he seems both proud and ashamed. All the while he courts the approval of readers whose racial attitudes are apt to be as muddled as his own: "If it had pleased Providence to drown any white men with them, and to let me know it, beyond a doubt I had rushed in. . . ." If anyone laughs, it will be at the narrator; if anyone gets angry, it will be at him, too. Bidding for sympathy, he only alienates the reader.

But the rogue's bigoted point of view becomes a way of exposing contradictions in more minds than his own. Humanitarianism and bigotry can coexist in an individual as well as in a culture, and Blackmore shows that the problem is not the monopoly of a vulgar Welshman. At the inquest following the shipwreck, the most blatant racism comes from an English coroner: "I never sate on a black man yet, and I won't sit on a black man now . . . I'll not disgrace his Majesty's writ by sitting upon damned niggers" (68). If the attitude behind his speech is more ugly than comic, it was not un-English in 1782 or in 1872, when other Victorians besides Blackmore wrote with a sense of national as well as racial superiority. His eighteenth-century Welshman thinks in the same terms as many of his Victorian English readers, but Davy's special and unconscious gift is to make racism seem ludicrous.

From an Anglo-Saxon point of view, he is silly enough for taking pride in being Welsh. But when he claims to be a descendant of King David without a taint of "Jewish blood" (142), he carries faith in ancestry to absurd lengths, and eventually makes his racism an affront to English self-esteem. It would be one thing to assume with David that the English are superior to the French ("Frogs," "Crappos"), but quite something else to read that the Welsh are superior to both (469). Though a recent Welsh critic thinks that Blackmore agreed with Davy on this point,[18] other evidence suggests a wide gap between the views of the narrator and the author. In *Cradock Nowell*, nations were scolded for claiming to be the "favoured child of God" (347); and war, which Davy thinks is "so good for us" (347), is considered a thing worse than cannibalism. David's opinions need to be measured against his dismissal of the New Testament as the "weaker" part of the Bible. He dislikes it because, with the exception of St. Paul and St. Peter ("who cut the man's ear off"), it exhibits "nobody of a patriotic spirit" (431).

This last opinion could prove the most distressing of all for the Victorian patriot who wanted to distance himself from the reprehensible Welshman. Where any conflict arose between imperialism and Christianity, the patriotic response was to ignore it, not to exploit it after the fashion of the Quaker politician John Bright or the pious Gladstone. Certainly one was not to offend piety in David's way by putting down the New Testament. With this tactless reprobate expressing some of the less defensible attitudes of the age, no wonder the *Examiner* told Blackmore to write his next novel in the third person. To represent life from an alien viewpoint was an "annoying" mistake. And so was his choice of subject matter: "I lived three and a half years in Wales," Mrs. Mortimer Collins told Blackmore, "so I learnt the character of the Welsh, and I despise the people so much that I think they are not worth writing about."[19]

II   Alice Lorraine *and the Retreat from Tragedy*

Who were worth writing about? Obviously Mrs. Collins considered the English worthy, and of them perhaps the worthiest were the landed gentry, the indispensable people for scores of Victorian novels. Blackmore had started out with the gentry in *Clara Vaughan* and *Cradock Nowell,* almost escaped from them in *Lorna Doone,* and glimpsed them only through the Welshman's vulgar eyes in *The Maid of Sker.* Now he returned to the rural aristocracy for his new novel, focusing on the imagined Gothic manor of Coombe Lorraine, set high on the Sussex Downs west of Steyning, near the villages of Washington and Wiston.[20] But the setting was to be expansive, with shifts in scene to London where Hilary, the irresponsible young heir of the Lorraines, plays at studying law before visiting the cherry orchards of Kent and falling in love with a farmer's daughter. Eventually he would go to Spain to fight with Wellington's army in episodes based upon Sir William F. Napier's *History of the War in the Peninsula and in the South of France.* So wide a perspective demanded that Blackmore write from an omniscient viewpoint, even though his one previous attempt at this kind of narrative had resulted in the sprawling incoherence of *Cradock Nowell.* This early failure was a bad omen, for now he was attempting something that called for all the skill and concentration at his command.

Alice Lorraine was to be a tragedy, a rare thing in Victorian fiction before the major novels of Thomas Hardy. Blackmore intended the plot to turn upon the character of young Hilary, who in spite of his honor and affectionate good nature was to become "the ruin of his friends."[21] This plan raised difficulties from the outset. Blackmore's verse tragedy twenty years earlier had evolved from the impassioned flaws of King Eric, a mature if psychotic character; but what tragedy could come from the pranks of a nobleman's son who throws darts in a barrister's chambers and mounts a market wagon at Covent Garden to sell carrots and cauliflowers? In the lamest of puns, Blackmore complained that Hilary's role was "a hard one to unroll."[22] Struggling with difficulties of his own choosing, he started the story five times before mailing the first number to Blackwood in January 1874. The novel began appearing in *Blackwood's* in March and continued—with a gap in November after the author complained of overwork—through the following April.

The unfolding story creates a strange discord between the underlying plot and the texture of description and dialogue. The graceful Sussex landscapes, the earthy talk of Bottler the pig-man, the gusto of the sporting parson Struan Hales (who would have sworn more vehemently had Blackwood not objected), and the pranks of Hilary launch the novel upon a bright surface of summer vigor and playfulness. Even the borrowings from Gothic fiction are sketched in lightly, as if the comet of 1811 and the prophecy by a long-dead astrologer were matters of "mere superstition" (24). But the omens are essential to the tragic design. The prophecy of crisis comes true as Hilary quarrels with his scornful father and leaves the house to fight the French in Spain. His sister Alice now begins to assume tragic responsibilities, and her pride and severity suggest a role like Antigone's once she learns that a maiden must offer her life to save the falling house. When an old woman tells how a stream called the Woeburn breaks out of the hillside in a time of danger, the heroine cannot quite dismiss the final words as superstition: "Only this can save Lorraine,/One must plunge to rescue twain" (115).

The tragic design is furthered by the movement of the plot from a June beginning toward a bitter winter of crisis. Autumn reminds a man that "light is surely waning, and the darkness gathering in"; it also reminds the narrator of the need to bring his dark forshadowings to a tragic fulfillment. Referring specifically to one character's scheming, he notes that "it is high time to work, to strengthen the threads of the wavering plan, to tighten the mesh of the woven web, to cast about here and there for completion—if the design shall be ever complete" (135).[23] The words suggest Blackmore's anxieties about following his own "wavering plan" to its intended end. As the presence of a village sibyl might suggest, his plan was to force the heroine into a dilemma such as Lucy Ashton faces in Sir Walter Scott's *Bride of Lammermoor*, one of the few impressive tragic English novels before Hardy's *Return of the Native*. Lucy has to choose between marrying a rake or staying loyal to the man who loves her; Alice will have to marry a rake or die. She reads Scott's *Lady of the Lake* (298) while troubles gather around her and the Woeburn begins flowing down the hillside. By now, Hilary has fallen into disgrace by losing a huge sum of government monies in Spain. To raise funds to cover the loss, Alice must marry for money or find a way to die, no mortgage on the estate being possible while she is living. She agrees to be married, but on the night before the wedding she walks through the snow toward the black waters of the Woeburn, seeking death "with a firmer step than a bride's towards a bridegroom." Then, "commending her soul to God in good Christian manner, and without a fear, or tear, or sigh," she commits "her body to the Death-bourne" (356).

At this point the distressed novelist wrote his publisher asking what to do. Complaining on the same day of having to keep up with the schedule of serial publication, he told another writer that he was "in the anguish of polishing off" his heroine.[24] But to John Blackwood he suggested an alternative:

> Herewith comes part XI corrected. Alice is to go a smash in the Woeburn, as intended ab initio, & foretold by the Astrologer. It has always been meant for a Tragedy, & by the sacrifice of her life all are saved.
> However I know that the public hate tragedies; & it is just possible to rescue her, if compatible with good art. And I feel that so much light writing has crept in, that I hesitate as to the final darkness.—Pray give me your opinion, & Mrs. Blackwood's [if she kindly reads it], & your good nephew's.—If you are unanimous against the fatal result, there is time to vary it, if you let me know speedily.
> I hope you are quite rid of cold.   (20 January 1875)

This note marks the zenith (or the nadir) of his efforts to please the publisher and the readers of a first-rate magazine. Knowing that "the public hate tragedies," he must also have known that John Blackwood nonetheless accepted the drowning of an earlier heroine in George Eliot's *Mill on the Floss,* published but not serialized by the firm in 1860. Then Blackwood had written that "the greatest lovers of all ending happily must admit that Providence [i.e., George Eliot] was kind in removing Maggie. She could not have been happy here."[25] But if Blackmore's heroine could be rescued she might yet find happiness. She had just met a likely husband, and the astrologer's locked box might contain treasure to redeem the family fortunes. With these options, the crisis in the narrative was also a crisis of choice for the author, who spent at least one January day hesitating before the "final darkness."

He did not quite surrender responsibility to the Blackwoods. His next letter announced a decision: "Alice has been pulled out again, as I quite perceived & anticipated the force of your remarks that the general tone of the story does not lead to intense blackness. The next batch will be light & (I hope) pleasant reading" (27 February 1875). Reviving the apparently dead heroine, he returned to the

motif of rebirth in *Lorna Doone*, though this time the miraculous
event takes place in an oddly mundane setting. The maiden revives
at night beneath a tarpaulin spread over the courtyard where
Bottler has been butchering hogs. This unplanned episode has a
grotesque vitality, with embers glowing red against flint walls and
the ground steaming from melting frost. As a scene of rebirth, the
pig-man's courtyard even has some appropriateness, since pigs were
sacrificed in the mysteries at Eleusis, the animal dying "in place of
the initiand."[26] "I do believe we could make a flock of sheep out of
a row of flints" (372), says the Rev. Hales as he helps to bring the
unconscious heroine back to life. He succeeds, but her revival marks
the end of Blackmore's intended tragic novel. Rather than
emulating the *Antigone* of Sophocles, he only achieves a faint echo
of the awesome drama by Euripides of sacrificial death, rescue, and
renewal: Alice's homecoming through the snowdrifts to Coombe
Lorraine calls to mind "the pale return of Alcestis" (377).

Surprisingly, the reviewers had few complaints about the ending,
although the *Athenaeum* did consider it "a little far-fetched."[27]
Blackmore's friend James Davis in the *Saturday Review* recognized
the "difficult task" of acclimatizing "an Antigone or Alcestis on the
less heroic soil of English womanhood."[28] He noted without censure
the *deus ex machina* while commending the humor and the pastoral
scenes, admired also by Robert Louis Stevenson,[29] with their
suggestions of Theocritus and Horace. These echoes, not the intended parallels with Sophocles and Euripides, governed Davis's
view that *Alice Lorraine* "will sustain the reputation of one of our
best English novelists. Seldom have we come across so fresh and
pleasant a prose idyl."

But in spite of its praise as Blackmore's "best work" in 1875,[30] the
novel eventually shared the fate of all his books besides *Lorna
Doone*, and even his rare twentieth-century critics express little lik-
ing for it.[31] At the time, at least one person besides the author
realized that something had gone wrong. The outspoken Mrs.
Collins once more reported her reaction: "I kept saying to Mortimer
that I thought it by far the best book you had written. But as I went
on I thought it did not keep up so well. I am wondering whether
you got hurried over it."[32] She guessed the sense of defeat that
Blackmore had already expressed to Blackwood: "I do not think
that I shall ever attempt a full-length novel again. The strain on the
brain, & the trouble to keep clear, take too much fibre out of me"
(31 March 1875). He had tried too hard and achieved too little. In

his fiftieth year, he was ready to quit a frustrating profession.

III   Cripps, the Carrier *and* Erēma

Blackmore's resolve to stop writing novels lasted barely two months. By May 1875 he was at work on a new one, and eight more would follow before his death in 1900. But for a time he did lower his sights. The next two books were shorter and much less ambitious than *Alice Lorraine;* they were also less favorably received. That they ever reached the public is surprising, given Blackmore's legal battles and ill health following the alleged suicide of his brother Henry Turberville in August 1875. Fighting for a share of Henry's fortune, which in three different wills was designated for (1) a Yeovil chemist and his daughter, (2) the erection of a statue of Shakespeare, and (3) the notorious atheist and radical politician Charles Bradlaugh,[33] Blackmore was at the same time defending himself against a libel suit for charging that his brother had been poisoned. Goaded by the prospect of paying heavy damages, he survived rheumatism, bronchitis, and slight paralysis 'while finishing *Cripps, the Carrier*, which ran from 1 January through 10 June 1876 in the popular illustrated weekly the *Graphic* and appeared across the Atlantic in *Harper's*. The double serialization was a sign of his new prestige and a bulwark against the threat of financial ruin.

Despite the turmoil during its composition, this modest "Woodland Tale" is the most simply written and relaxed of Blackmore's novels. Set mainly in the countryside around Oxford, the action covers only the months from December 1837 to the following May, roughly the time of year spanned by the serial in the *Graphic*. The seasons give a pattern to the narrative much as they do to Hardy's earlier woodland idyll, *Under the Greenwood Tree* (1872), a book which Blackmore deeply admired and probably read before he finished *Cripps*.[34] The two novelists met at the Saville Club on 17 April 1875; Hardy visited Gomer House on May 4 and soon wrote his letter in praise of *Lorna Doone;* "A kindred sentiment between us in so many things is, I suppose, partly because we both spring from the West of England."[35] Blackmore in turn became a Hardy enthusiast: "There are very few novels I can read, but his I never miss."[36] He set *Cripps* in roughly the same era as *Under the Greenwood Tree*, opened it at the same time of year, and focused on the same rural occupation, the job of a "tranter," or carrier, who carts goods from village to village along the woodland roads. Both works are pastoral comedies, most alive in framed scenes of rustic dialogue and moving at a cart-horse's pace toward summer and the celebration of marriage. But the world of Blackmore's story is complicated by Oxford, with its shrewd lawyers and tradesmen and its gowned followers of John Henry Newman during the Tractarian effort to affirm the catholic origin and mission of the English Church. As a place of controversy, Oxford invited comedy with a bit of satiric sting, and Blackmore—smarting from courtroom skirmishes—prefaced the book with a boastful epigraph from *The Wasps*, the satire by Aristophanes upon compulsive legalism: "Our little subject is not wanting in sense; it is well within your capacity and at the same time cleverer than many vulgar comedies."[37]

Although the tone of *Cripps* is comic, it further differs from *Under the Greenwood Tree* in its "absurd" melodramatic plot, which, the *Spectator* insisted, has nothing to do with "the charm of the story."[38] Where Hardy lets things develop through a series of "Dutch pictures," Blackmore takes an early plunge into mystery. The squire's daughter, Grace Oglander, vanishes on a dark December day; and at nightfall a frightened girl witnesses the burial of a woman in a frozen quarry at Headington. The situation recalls the presumed death of the heroine in *The Woman in White*, but no one in *Cripps* has read Collins's novel, and the villagers assume the worst, doubting the wisdom of providence. Since Blackmore plays providence within the story, the reader can be fairly certain that Grace is not dead: grace is never dead in his novels. After the first spring thaw, she turns up in the budding woods, waiting to be discovered. Evil in the meantime works itself out of Blackmore's universe through the self-destructive career of the lawyer who planned her abduction. Believing that he has killed his well-loved son, the lawyer commits a grisly suicide. Even in a pastoral mood, Blackmore cannot do without melodrama.

But the essential movement of the absurd plot is the myth of Persephone, unfolding once more with the passing of winter. Freed from her captor, Grace returns to her father's house by the end of May. Her guide is the stalwart middle-aged Cripps, the comic hero, who brings the lost one back from supposed death and prepares the squire for a homely scene of recognition:

"Now, doth your Worship know that all things cometh in a round, like a sound cart-wheel, to all such folks as trusts the Lord?"

"I know that you have such a theory, Cripps. You beat the whole village in theology."

"And the learned scholar in Oxford, your Worship; he were quite doubled up about the tribe of Levi. But for all of their stuff, the Lord still goeth on, making His rounds to His own right time; and now His time hath come for you, Squire."[39]

Grace's return completes the cycle of loss and recovery, leaving the once skeptical villagers of Beckley to talk now about a "miracle" (402).

Within the "round" of this movement, three other restorations take place, each consisting of a young man's return from the brink of death. One revival is intentionally comic, even Aristophanic. The victim in this case is the ascetic Tractarian clergyman, Thomas Hardenow—the "learned scholar" whom Cripps scorned for not seeing how Newman's views on celibacy would have affected the priestly tribe of Levi: "They must all a' died out in the first generation; if 'em ever come to any generation at all" (221). Hardenow's ordeal purges him of asceticism. Left gagged and tied on the floor of a hog shed (while he should be leading undergraduates through *Prometheus Bound)*, he is brought to consciousness by Cripps' lovely young sister. After twenty spoonfuls of soup, he vows to give up fasting; after thirty, he sees in the woman's "smiling eyes . . . the clearest and truest solution of his 'postulates on celibacy' " (413). With the fall of this ideal, the community within the novel is itself ready for renewal through the celebration of marriage. Even Cripps considers giving up bachelorhood. But he leaves the decision to his old horse:

"Thou shalt zettle it, Dobbin," he cried, leaning over and stroking his gingery loins. "It consarneth thee most, or, leastways, quite as much. Never hath any man had a better horse. The will of the Lord takes the strength out of all of us; but He leaveth, and addeth to the wisdom therein. Dobbin, thou seest things as never men can tell of. Now, if thou waggest thy tail to the right—I will; and so be to the left—I wun't. Mind what thou doest now. Call upon they wisdom, nag, and give thy master honestly the sense of thy discretion."

With a settled mind, and no disturbance, he awaited the delivery of Dobbin's tail. A fly settled on the white foam of the harness of the off side of this ancient horse. Away went his tail with a sprightly flick at it; and Cripps accepted the result. (419)

Cripps is acting with perfect consistency, for he has always maintained that "there be no such thing as luck. . . . The Lord in heaven is the master of us!" (108). The novel enacts his theology, questioning it at times, but leading to the conclusion expressed by Kenneth Budd: "Destiny in this village, in strong contrast to what it is generally doing in Hardy's Wessex, is working always towards the triumph of simple and persevering righteousness."[40] But Blackmore's providence makes no one a puppet, not even Dobbin, who is left free to exercise "discretion" (according to Cripps), and it works with the extra grace of a sense of humor.

With its woodlands, rustics, and gypsies, the book merits the comment "Wordsworth in prose" and the praise it received as a "village idyll."[41] Although the best scenes are of people talking in the neighborhood inn or the squire's kitchen, Blackmore has only restrained, not lost, his powers of description. With the microscopic detail of Ruskin or Hopkins, he catches a puddle of water in the act of freezing. What other eye has seen the "little splinters (held as are the ribs and harl of feathers) spreading, and rising like stems of lace"; and who else has heard the "smooth, crisp jostle" of these crystals "sinking, as the wind flew over them, into the quavering consistence of a coverlet of ice" (9)? Or description can blend with meditation in the manner of Barnes or Hardy as Blackmore reflects on the variety of wheel-ruts along a country road. Each one "has a voice of its own" (164), like the various trees in the wind at the start of *Under the Greenwood Tree*. The quiet style keeps inviting reflection on nature and human nature, providence, marriage, and possibly on the topic that inspired this letter to the author: "Sir, From several passages in last Saturday's installment [apparently Chapter XXV] . . . I infer that you have perceived the change that has been coming about in the status of women—moreover, that you perceive it without displeasure, perhaps with approval." The writer, Eliza M. Lynch, was hesitant with good reason: "One is prone to see what one wishes to see," she admitted, before asking Blackmore to sign a petition for extending the franchise to women householders. Given his conservatism, he probably did not sign, but he saved the letter. Whatever he thought of her politics, he must have approved her taste: "I can not tell you how much I admire your writing, which is so picturesque and true to nature—careful writing, meant to be pondered at leisure. . . ."[42]

As a picture of village life, *Cripps, the Carrier* points toward

Blackmore's later achievement in *Christowell* and *Perlycross*, his full-scale studies in the workings of a rural community. But the *Academy* found the setting too narrow ("a corner of Oxfordshire"), and the author reported that his critics "abused" the book. Negotiating with Leslie Stephen for the publication of his next novel in the *Cornhill Magazine*, he felt sufficiently under a cloud to ask that it appear anonymously. Stephen assured him that his name was "most certainly a good one" and added some sound advice: "Your popularity depends upon the merits of your writing, & if you are now and then judged harshly, as all popular authors are, I don't think you need care about it, unless a critic may incidentally give a useful hint or two. You have been worried lately, as you told me, & are doubtless more sensitive than usual . . . ."[43] Blackmore responded by following one critical hint too literally, for he abandoned the theme of rural community in his new novel, *Erēma* and expanded the setting to include California and Virginia. The book turned out to be a study in isolation, written from the viewpoint of a young woman who has no family and knows no community.

Her name, "Erema," means lost and desolate. In the epigraph, it appears in lines from Sophocles's tragedy of Heracles and his bride, Deianira, a woman "gone from her mother/ like a calf that is lost."[44] But like *Alice Lorraine, Erēma* is another evasion of tragedy. More precisely, it is a story of what happens after a tragic family catastrophe. The terrible main event, over before the story begins, foreshadows the action that Dostoyevsky soon would dramatize in *The Brothers Karamazov:* an illegitimate son commits parricide, and the legitimate son, Erēma's father, receives the blame for the murder. After losing her mother, brother, and sisters in infancy, the heroine sees her father die on a mountainside in California at the start of the novel. This event proves to be the last hard shock of tragedy; all that remains are reverberations, felt in narratives of past events while she tries to find the murderer and clear her father's name. Tragic reverberations have to be absorbed, and that is essentially Erēma's story.

The ease with which she absorbs them and achieves her goal limits the interest of a novel which lacks the humor, the memorable rustic characters, and the lively natural detail of Blackmore's best writing. The American critic who called it his "greatest work"[45] must have been thinking less of its intrinsic merits than of the compliment to his own nation when the heroine renounces her English title and comes back to settle in the United States. Most readers were unimpressed, perhaps because the clichés in the plot were by now too familiar: "the library subscribers knew the whole mixture and were becoming allergic to it."[46] The most telling criticism charged Blackmore with the "purely negative" aim of achieving "absolute harmlessness": the characters "always do what they ought to do, and think what they ought to think." The reviewer wished that Erēma would "do something wrong, even by accident."[47]

Blackmore was trapped by his own burgeoning respectability. From the start he had tried to dissociate his work from the allegedly immoral sensation novels, and he had recently won praise for portraying "wholesome English girlhood" and offering "pleasing samples of what we should like our daughters and nieces to be." To highly respectable readers, these portraits were all the more welcome for coming at a time when "so many authors" seemed "in league to propagate a bad pattern."[48] English fiction after Dickens was splitting into at least three main camps, consisting of safe family reading, lurid thrillers, and serious problem novels like George Eliot's *Daniel Deronda* or Hardy's *Return of the Native*. These last were not designed for the ubiquitous Victorian Young Person. Though Blackmore had insisted that "if a book is to be read aloud by young ladies, it shd. be written by them,"[49] he was caught now in a wave of reaction against the new boldness in depicting vice. Having asked Mrs. Collins what she thought of Hardy, he felt the force of this reaction in her reply. She was an expert at bowdlerizing her husband Mortimer's novels, and she obviously thought that *Far from the Madding Crowd* deserved censorship:

I read up to the part where there is [the] scene of the coffin and the woman & her illegitimate child in it. I had been disgusted all along, but when I came to that I threw down the book and would not read another word.

I think I never saw a more unwholesome disgusting *beastly* (excuse such language in indignation) book. It is a *forced* style all through. There is an attempt to imitate George Eliot in drawing character and *you* in scenery & nature. I don't like George Eliot—she is too morbid, but Hardys [sic] imitation of her is horrid. I would never read a line of any other book by that man. I was hoping a few years ago, when people seemed to like your books and others of a healthy character, that a better taste in literature was appearing—but the "Cornhill" and two or three other papers have done their best to keep up unwholesome literature.[50]

Blackmore's own tastes were not so squeamish, but in praising Hardy's novel he called parts of it "revolting."[51] He cared "very little" for George Eliot's later fiction, and preferred one of "Mrs.

Braddon's golden-haired homicidals" to Gwendolen Harleth in
Daniel Deronda. He had an opposite criticism of the hero, "a prig
of the first water," and wondered if the character got "antenuptially
circumcised" but did not read on to find out.[52] Henry James seemed
cold to him; George Meredith apparently was for him as for many
others the "great unintelligible."[53] But these writers became the
winners of a new literary respectability that outlasted his own Victorian fame. By 1895, Blackmore was already suffering from the
changes in public taste: "I am threatened with a sad collapse. The
sale of my novels has dropped almost to the vanishing point. It is
the same with Wm. Black's & all the other Veterans who have not
rushed into Pornography, or Psychics, or Diabology, or Anti-
Christianity, or something else that 'catches on.' "[54]

Of course, blaming "corrupted taste" was too easy an excuse for
the novelist's own failures of will and imagination. Blackmore com-
promised from the start in his dealing with Blackwood, grumbling
about editorial prudery but accepting the "necessity" of accom-
modation (16 January 1872). He had rescued a heroine partly on the
grounds that the public "hate tragedies." To write fiction that
would deserve to survive the shifts in tastes of his era, he would
need to let his characters make mistakes and suffer the conse-
quences. They could not, so long as his authorial providence stayed
as protective as it had been in *Erēma*. As if sensing the problem, he
withdrew a bit of his protectiveness in his next novel and lapsed a
little from respectability. This time his characters err and suffer.
The stubborn heroine resists the law and quarrels with her parents;
the romantic hero is a smuggler who provides the occasion for the
death of a likable captain of the coast guard. Their forgotten story
deserves to rank near *Lorna Doone* among the better romances of
the century.

CHAPTER 5

Mary Anerley *and the Novels of Rural Community*

> When he has refreshed his memory with the map of England, let any man point out upon it, if he can deliberately, any two parishes he knows well, which he can also certify to be exactly like each other. . . . Each place has its own style, and tone, vein of sentiment, and lines of attitude, deepened perhaps by the lore and store of many generations.[1]

PUBLISHED on both sides of the Atlantic in 1879 - 80, *Mary Anerley* heralded a decade of high literary adventure. *Treasure Island, King Solomon's Mines,* and *She* were soon to follow, and the trend set by Stevenson and Rider Haggard would continue in the next decade with Anthony Hope's *Prisoner of Zenda* and John Falkner's *Moonfleet,* a story based like Blackmore's upon the exploits of English smugglers. But unlike these romances, *Mary Anerley* keeps close to shore and the daily lives of ordinary villagers. This "Yorkshire Tale" mingles adventure with the common experience of farmers, fisherfolk, clergymen, lawyers, innkeepers—a Dickensian swarm of characters who far outnumber the smugglers and their enemies, the ever-bumbling coast guard. Compared to the streamlined, suspenseful narratives of Stevenson and Haggard, Blackmore's moves as ponderously as a broad-beamed trading ship, hauling a heavy cargo. But his attention to ordinary life provides a solid context for adventure, and the weight of the book—most of it—is a sign of considerable treasure. Not since *Lorna Doone* had he shaped as rich a substance into so artful a form, revealing unexpected skill in drawing simultaneous lines of action toward a satisfactory if predictable end. The conventions governing the plot are still those of romance, but the style and the portrayal of a village community have a distinctive richness, while the scenes of humor and pathos approach the strange realism of Dickens.

Written with more than his "usual care" at the maximum rate of

81

one page a day,[2] the story grew out of a Yorkshire holiday with his wife at Bridlington and Flamborough in the late summer of 1877. The title and a faint image of the heroine came from a poem by his friend Arthur Munby, whose "Mary Anerley" appeared in *Macmillan's* (March 1866) along with an installment of *Cradock Nowell*. Blackmore dedicated the novel to Munby, perhaps more for his help with dialect and setting than for his verses describing a beautiful girl in love with a sailor named Robin. The novelist still had the task of selecting a time for the story, of setting it along the bold chalk cliffs of Flamborough and on the moorlands of upper Teesdale, and of giving Mary a respectable farm family while making Robin a smuggler with no family at all. He created the outlaw-hero from the legendary figure of Robin Lyth, a smuggler in some accounts, a buccaneer or a shipwrecked sailor in others: his cave is found beside the North Landing at Flamborough. With this much established, the plot could work out the ancient business of revealing the hero's identity, while he plays the role of a seafaring Robin Hood, for whom a notorious smuggler's bay is named farther up the Yorkshire coast.

The double theme of identity and outlawry is announced in Blackmore's epigraph. In Book III of *The Odyssey*, Nestor questions his unknown visitors, young Telemachus and his companions:

> Who are you, strangers? Where are you sailing from,
> and where to, down the highways of sea water?
> Have you some business here? or are you, now,
> reckless wanderers of the sea, like those corsairs
> who risk their lives to prey on other men?[3]

Transferred to the novel, these questions point directly to the outlaw Robin Lyth, who knows nothing of his origins and tries to make up for anonymity by winning fame as a smuggler. Trying to "work his own name out," Robin has sought adventure since boyhood "simply because he had no name."[4] As a young man, he rejects the common task of fishing, the trade of his foster-father, for the glamour, excitement, and money of smuggling (which Blackmore, gibing at the Liberals' economic policies, calls "Free Trade"). A "reckless wanderer," with less of the dutiful Telemachus in him than the daring of Odysseus, Robin is driven to "rejoice in danger, having very little else to rejoice in" (73). But the allusion to *The*

Odyssey promises an end to wandering and a deepening of the hero's sense of identity and purpose.

Although missing heirs are always turning up in Victorian fiction, Blackmore ingeniously develops the motif through the four simultaneous quests that constitute the plot. Robin pursues Mary, whose parents object to having a smuggler for a son-in-law; the coast guard pursues Robin, and so does his noble father, returning from India to investigate the possibility that his son is still alive. The fourth quest is negative, with the usurping holders of the estate trying to keep it out of the hands of the rightful heir. The plot achieves a concentration of focus unusual in Blackmore by opening virtually *in medias res* in July 1801, when the twenty-year-old mystery of Robin's identity is within months of being solved. After a grim prologue, the early chapters contrast the austere setting of Scargate Hall, near the mountain pass, or "scaur gate" leading into Westmoreland, with the fruitful Anerley Farm just across the "Dane's Dyke" from Flamborough. At Scargate, the harshness of the Yordas family is reflected in the landscape and enacted through a history of conflict between fathers and sons. Litigation forms a part of this history, and so does a feudal sort of sexual exploitation, sanctioned by the custom of naming the master's eldest illegitimate son "Jordas" and giving him the post of "dogman" (17). As the novel begins, Scargate Hall is the opposite of Anerley Farm, where no lawyers come, no fathers cast away their sons, and the land passes with "judicious give-and-take" down through the generations. Hall and farm polarize the Yorkshire universe of the novel.

But the contrast lessens as the story grows. Farmer Anerley is disappointed in his sons, and his petted daughter Mary has inherited his stubborn will, "which makes against perfection" (27). She offends both parents by falling in love with a young outlaw whose possible illegitimacy prompts this outburst from her mother: "To think that a child of mine, my one and only daughter, who looks as if butter wouldn't melt in her mouth, should be hand-in-glove with the wickedest smuggler of the age, the rogue everybody shoots at, but cannot hit him, because he was born to be hanged—the by-name, the by-word, the by-blow, Robin Lyth!" (99). Her father's still fiercer reaction spreads the theme of parental hostility from the hall to the once-idyllic farmhouse. But romance, by a nice balance, now springs up on the moors around Scargate where the pampered adolescent, Lancelot "Pet" Carnaby," the supposed heir to the estate, falls in love with a Wordsworthian maiden called "Insie of the Gill." He begins reading the *Lyrical Ballads* of "that bold young man over the mountains" who is "trying to turn poetry upside down, by making it out of every single thing he sees" (166). The spoiled boy of the hall is himself touched by poetry while Mary and the outlaw with the gold earrings face a wintry trial after a short Yorkshire summer of romance.

The darker turn to the story comes through Lieutenant Carraway's efforts to capture the smugglers. The father of seven children, with another one on the way, this poor officer of the coast guard is at once comic and tragic, a profane man who calls his motley underlings sons of bitches in the vicar's presence (109) and later browbeats one of them into a fatal urge for revenge. Pride is Carraway's flaw, and he shares with the tragic Oedipus a hasty tongue as well as a limping walk, for his boney ramrod figure is marred by a split heel. But in devotion to wife and family, he plays the role of a homely, beleaguered Hector, risking his life to capture the outlaw and win the much-needed bounty of £100. The story of his family affection contrasts with the romances on the moor and along the coast, bringing into the novel a deeper dimension of love—one "worthier of attention than the flitting fancy of boy and girl, who pop upon one another, and skip through zig-zag vernal ecstasy, like the weathery dalliance of gnats" (178).

The contrast between the true and the untried kinds of love makes for one great comic scene when Carraway, in the line of duty, tries to ambush Mary and Robin during their happiest evening of courtship. But Carraway's "Preventive Force," enjoying the lovers' talk from behind a hedge, fails miserably at preventing romance, and Carraway must try once again to capture the young outlaw. When winter comes, he leaves home on his last quest, humbly reenacting Hector's farewell to Andromache in Book VI of *The Iliad*. After the usual complaints from Mrs. Carraway about his pipe-smoking, she finds words for the real worry that preys upon her mind:

"Charles, I cannot bear your going. The weather is so dark and the sea so lonely, and the waves are making such a melancholy sound. It is not like the summer nights, when I can see you six miles off, with the moon upon the sails, and the land out of the way. Let anybody catch him that has the luck. Don't go this time, Charley."

Carraway kissed his wife and sent her to the baby, who was squalling well upstairs. And when she came down he was ready to start, and she brought the baby for him to kiss.

"Good-bye, little chap—good-bye, dear wife." With his usual vigour and flourish, he said, "I never knew how to kiss a baby; though I have had such a lot of them." (222 - 23)

These are his last moments with his wife. He will be brought home dead, and winter will find his family starving inside the frozen cottage, with the baby dead in his widow's arms.

At this snowy time of the story, life reaches its lowest point, as if providence has ceased to care. "There is no God," Mrs. Carraway tells her children as her breasts go dry, and the narrator does not qualify her statement (343). But in the most unlikely of characters, an annoyingly talkative "factor" or land agent whose name means "biting," providence has an agent, too. Mordacks's quest for the missing heir parallels the ill-fated one of Lieutenant Carraway, and it brings him from York to Flamborough in time to rescue Carraway's family. Mordacks's charity creates another dimension of love to go with the contrast between romantic eros and domestic affection. The shrewd agent becomes a second St. Oswald, the patron of the Flamborough church, as he emulates the Northumbrian king who sent his dinner in a silver dish to feed the poor and then ordered that the dish be broken and divided among them. Mordacks provides food and warmth for the stricken family, left to starve while snow drifts against their cottage door. His example stirs the dormant "kindness of the neighbours" (346), and by Christmas the story has taken an upward turn.

Coldness of both heart and weather makes life terrible for Mrs. Carraway and her children before Mordacks comes, and coldness is the common element in three separate ordeals for the young men in the novel. For each, the ordeal is part of an initiation. After Carraway's death in a sea-cave, Robin swims at night through chilling waters and then roams the land as a fugitive accused of murder. He leaves behind the smuggler's role and moves toward a more responsible sense of identity. His counterpart, the insolent youth at Scargate Hall, suffers wounded pride and bleeding hands on the snowy moor before seeing the girl Insie beside her own hearth-fire, looking so much like a "goddess" that his patronizing view of her must give way to a vision of wonder (305). Finally, in the most spectacular ordeal, Jordas the "dogman" almost smothers in a snowdrift at Stormy Gap. Rescued and cared for, the servant loses the bitterness of thinking that he matters less to the world than a good horse. With Robin and Lancelot Carnaby, he finds answers to questions of identity and purpose like those aimed at Telemachus in *The Odyssey*.

But unlike the epic, the novel shows no reunion of father and son. After the parricide in *Erēma*, the father's near murder of his son in *Cripps*, and the casting out of disgraced sons in *Alice Lorraine, The Maid of Sker*, and *Cradock Nowell*, Blackmore may have felt unequal to the task of resolving so deep-seated a conflict in his fiction. Fathers and sons would continue to be at odds in *Christowell* and *Springhaven;* atonement would come only toward the foreground in the last two novels of his old age. Without showing the expected reunion, *Mary Anerley* nonetheless achieves the end of romantic comedy, with forgiveness, reconciliation and the promise of marriages in the spring. Marriage restores the wanderers to the community of life, the theme underlying the whole novel and its portrayal of three kinds of love that build and restore relationships.

Community in a national sense dominates a late patriotic chapter on Trafalgar, but most of the story develops the theme in local terms by showing what the people in one small neighborhood have in common. The people of Flamborough share customs, a distinctive dialect, personal histories, and the dangers and rewards of harvesting the "fishful sea" (58). The launching of their fishing fleet on St. Swithin's Day makes one of the best communal scenes, alive with the predawn stir along the steep cove, the North Landing, that serves Flamborough as a harbor:

Here was a medley, not of fisher-folk alone, and all their bodily belongings, but also of the thousand things that have no soul, and get kicked about and sworn at much, because they cannot answer. Rollers, buoys, nets, kegs, swabs, fenders, blocks, buckets, kedges, corks, buckiepots, oars, poppies, tillers, spirits, gaffs, and every kind of gear (more than Theocritus himself could tell) lay about, and rolled about, and upset their own masters, here and there and everywhere, upon this half-acre of slip and stumble, at the top of the boat-channel down to the sea, and in the faint rivalry of three vague lights, all making darkness visible. (59)

This passage is more than a *tour de force*. Naming the fishing-gear is a way of evoking the complex working-life of the village culture. At the same time, the allusion to Theocritus's *Idyll XXI*, in which an old man dreams of landing a golden fish, prepares for the discovery of the infant hero, clothed in white linen with gold buttons and lying asleep by a fishing boat. Like the similar episode in

The Maid of Sker, this lucky find by a childless man lifts the narrative into the realm of myth, whether it calls to mind Dictys, who nets the box containing Perseus, or Terynon, the Welsh farmer who finds a royal infant swaddled in silk outside his stable in *The Mabinogian.* The gift of fresh life can do with fine wrappings and the shine of gold. But the novel balances the mythic aura of the discovery with the neighbors' crude bit of humor. Left by the fisherman in the care of Granny Pegler, the little boy sleeps beside her on the brow of the hill as the "lavings" of the village, the women, children, and old men, climb up from the shore:

"Nanny Pegler, got oop wi' ye!" cried a woman even older, but of tougher constitution. "Shame on ye to lig aboot so. Be ye browt to bed this toime o' life?"

"A wonderful foine babby for sich an owd moother!" another proceeded with the elegant joke; "and foine swaddles too, wi' solid gowd upon 'em!" (62)

These are the voices of communal people who must share their bit of fun in spite of hard work and the sudden intrusion of mythic reality into familiar life.

The villagers surround the romantic story with intimations of a culture that has more riches than any realm of literary convention. Their world has conventions of its own, like the custom an old woman recalls from her wedding day when the couple "sowed broad beans, like a pigeon's foot-tread, out and in, all the way to church" (182). Going to a bigger wedding, a bridegroom "put his oar into the sea and rowed from Flamborough all the way to Filey Brigg, with thirty-five fishermen after him; for the Flamborough people make a point of seeing one another through their troubles"; and everyone celebrated by burning seaweed on the beach before rowing home by moonlight (52). The sense of community is just as strong when the people work, whether netting shoals of mackeral or taking advantage of a rare sunny day to wash the clothes. This job goes on with the young daughters minding the infants and the mothers

plying hand and tongue, in a little field by the three cross roads, where the gaffers and gammers of bygone time had set up troughs of proven wood, and the bilge of a long storm-beaten boat, near a pool of softish water. Stout brown arms were roped with curd, and wedding-rings looked slippery things, and thumb-nails bordered with inveterate black, like broad beans ripe for planting, shone through a hubbub of snowy froth; while sluicing, and wringing, and rinsing went on, over the bubbled and lathery turf; and every handy bush or stub, and every tump of wiry grass was sheeted with white, like a ship in full sail, and shining in the sun-glare. (120)

Where the community is, there Blackmore's writing is most alive, most evocative of the forms of energy that keep the village going. Three basic expressions of human energy—ceremony, work, and recreation—come into this picture. The wedding rings mark the rites that join the men and women in their diverse undertakings. The fishermen nap while the wives drudge, but the work is a social occasion for the women and their daughters, who "had got all the babies to nurse, and their toes and other members to compare, and dandelion chains to make." Blending with these forms of human energy are the elements of nature: the pool of washing water, the earth, the bright air, and the fire of the sun. Though the people may be too busy to notice, the community of life on this afternoon at Flamborough includes man and nature, with the energies of both blending to get the washing done.

Blackmore's communal and comic sense saves *Mary Anerley* from its trite conventions, itemized by Rudyard Kipling in his epitaph for the three-volume Victorian novel The Three-Decker (1896):

Fair held our breeze behind us—'twas warm with lovers' prayers.
We'd stolen wills for ballast and a crew of missing heirs.
They shipped as Able Bastards till the Wicked Nurse confessed,
And they worked the old three-decker to the Islands of the Blest.
                    . . . .

I left 'em all in couples akissing on the decks.
I left the lovers loving and the parents signing cheques.
In endless English comfort by country-folk caressed,
I left the old three-decker at the Islands of the Blest. . . .[5]

The verses admirably summarize Blackmore's plot, but the "ballast" of the story is not its stolen wills. The steadying substance consists rather of the humor and the homely priorities of people like the innkeeper and his wife at Filey, who step outside their door to watch Carraway sail after the smugglers while his brave little boy rides back along the shore at night toward Flamborough: " 'The world goeth up, and the world goeth down,' said the lady with her arms akimbo; 'and the moon goeth over the whole of us, John; but to my heart I do pity poor folk, as canna count the time to have the sniff of their own blankets' " (261). Throughout the story, earthiness and humor count for more than suspense, which is interrupted by the boozy antics of two wooden-legged sailors and by the fate of an overly thirsty revenue officer, just before the scene of Carraway's death. As in Dickens, pain and humor keep company in this novel. Though ignored in the twentieth century, it was recognized in 1880 as a "comedy of the first class," a "remarkable book,"[6] the author's best "since *Lorna Doone*."[7] These judgments deserve attention, for Victorian critics had unusual practice in distinguishing excellent from mediocre fiction, and they had not been blind to Blackmore's faults. Despite a century of changing tastes, *Mary Anerley* may prove with the effort of rediscovery—or no effort at all for anyone with Kipling's tolerance for the conventions of the three-decker novel.

I   *Anxiety and Pastoral Nostalgia in* Christowell

After *Mary Anerley*, Blackmore went on to write three other distinguished novels in his last troubled decades. He also wrote three severely criticized ones; and in spite of the enormous sales of *Lorna Doone*, he sensed that his fortunes were sliding downhill. He faced two different sorts of competition. The "advanced" novelists such as Meredith, James, and Hardy made his work seem increasingly old-fashioned, while the new romance-spinners in the 1880s began beating him at his own game. "I fear that the Raw-head [*sic*] and bloody bones school outflourish me,"[8] he complained in 1888, after Stevenson and Haggard had captured the popular imagination with tales of pirates and African warriors. In contrast to their thrillers, Blackmore's best books from this period are slow-paced and pastoral. They belong to the school of regional fiction which George Eliot had helped to establish with *Adam Bede* (1859) and which he had entered in the 1860s. Hardy now led this school, followed by William Black (1841 - 98), the Highland novelist; Richard Jeffries (1848 - 87), whose main region was Wiltshire; the Rev. Sabine Baring-Gould (1834 - 1924), a recorder of West Country folklore; and Eden Phillpotts (1862 - 1960), who dedicated his first Dartmoor novel to Blackmore.

Writing his own Dartmoor novel in *Christowell* (1881), Blackmore focused this time upon communal experience rather than individual adventure. A change in the titles of his novels from the names of characters to the names of villages marks this shift of emphasis. Already important in his earlier fiction, the community provides the main subject for this Devon pastoral and for *Springhaven* (1887), a historical novel set on the Sussex coast during the threat of Napoleonic invasion. In both books, a vulnerable parish faces something as evil as the vilest cut-throat in *Treasure Island*, but far less easy for a pistol shot or sword thrust to destroy. Blackmore still has villains, but the threat to his pastoral worlds is more than any single character can embody.

His least successful book in the 1880s provides some background for the sense of menace in his novels of community. Specific reasons for his anxiety come to the surface in his long satiric fantasy upon Darwinism and socialism, *The Remarkable History of Sir Thomas Upmore* (1884), the story of a young man's education and eventual rise to a position in Parliament. The book is remarkable for very little besides the hero's defiance of the law of gravity (in scenes recalling George MacDonald's "Light Princess") and a foreign scientist's conviction that the human race, by sheer willpower, can evolve a tail: "I am ze first." This believer in "creative evolution," attacked by orthodox Darwinians who call his doctrine "fundamentally erroneous," can only erupt in negations: "I say nah, I say non, I say bosh!"[9] His words could summarize Blackmore's attitude toward the direction of political and intellectual life in this decade. It was an "age of sacrilege," he said in verses on the removal of Blundell's School from its original buildings to a new site outside Tiverton; "It dashes into forbidden ground; what it cannot understand, it hates. . . ."[10] The times seemed determined to upset him. Dismayed by Gladstone's return to power in 1880, he saw omens of doom in the decline of British agriculture, the talk of Home Rule for Ireland, the Liberal government's half-hearted support of the empire, the rise of socialism, the challenge of science to the ideal of a classical education, and the growing acceptance of Darwin's theory of evolution. Because the theory could be twisted to support the liberal belief in progress (Darwin spoke of "progress toward perfection" in his conclusion to *The Origin of Species*), it was bound to offend Blackmore, who became increasingly convinced that things were drifting in the opposite direction.

To combat Darwin's influence in the 1880's, when the theory was spreading to nonbiological fields of study and speculation, the novelist had almost no scientific weapons. But as an orchardman, he had seen too many bad crops to believe in evolution if the term meant "progress." Blights, droughts, and untimely frosts taught him to accept the view of Virgil's *Georgics:* "all things, sadly falling off, grow worse,/ Relapsing, tottering, under nature's curse" (I, 11. 232ff., Blackmore's translation). Corresponding with a minor scientist, Dr. J. M. Winn, he wrote that "*de*volution is nature's law; without aid, divine and human, nothing ever improves itself, so far as I can see of it; 'ill weeds grow apace'; the lowest form of life is toughest."[11] While he had little scientific evidence for this view, he could at least side with his old friend Sir Richard Owen (Professor Megalow in the satire) and argue that Darwin's evidence was also inadequate. From the first, Owen had claimed that *The Origin of Species* failed to present enough facts to account for evolution in terms of "natural selection" or "survival of the fittest"—a process which Darwin said "acts by competition."[12] Though Owen made dogmatic blunders in the ensuing controversy, he had challenged Darwin on his most controversial deduction—one which later scientists would qualify, and which acquired the ugliest political and economic implications once nations and capitalists began justifying their dominance in terms of the survival of the fittest. Though an imperialist himself, Blackmore long ago had condemned war in *Cradock Nowell* for providing evidence in support of Darwin's theory (347), based as it was on the view that all organisms are engaged in a struggle for survival. Now in the smoke of intellectual combat he saw Darwinism as one form of an arrogant rationalism out to destroy faith in a creative and guiding providence.

His portrait of Darwin as Professor Brachipod, "an infirm, and disabled old man, who was killing himself prematurely, by wanting to know too much" (II, 208), is not always hostile, and it follows Darwin's own self-revelation in the *Autobiography* (1876). Not in the dead scientist but in the movement called Darwinism, Blackmore thought he detected the monster of liberalism. The "enemy ramps like Apollyon, striding across the way,"[13] he told Dr. Winn, drawing an image from *Pilgrim's Progress*. In the frailest intellectual armor, he prepared to do battle. His preface to *Thomas Upmore* echoes the famous attack on modern rationalism in Newman's *Apologia* (Chapt. V), where "the wild living intellect of man" in its "suicidal excesses" appears as the enemy of the faith that sustains life. Newman asks what "face-to-face antagonist" can "withstand and baffle the fierce energy of passion and the all-corroding, all-dissolving skepticism of the intellect"; Blackmore asks what "power shall resist the wild valour of the man, who proves that his mind is a tadpole spawn, and then claims for that mind supreme dominion and inborn omniscience?" (iv).

Given the prestige of late-Victorian science, any effort to under-cut its confidence was apt to be quixotic. But a satirist might at least reawaken the humanistic concerns that science failed to satisfy. For Blackmore, the issue was not how things originate, which he con-fessed was beyond him, but why—why do things exist and develop? The question of ultimate origins and purposes was either being ig-nored by Darwinian theory or treated in a way that challenged faith in providence. Blackmore's humanism underlies the pages of awkward satire, particularly in defense of a classical education (a defense more gracefully accomplished by Matthew Arnold earlier in the decade), and it surfaces in a rare moment of clarity when a lady looks at an oak tree and puts a question to the young narrator:

"Who brought up this tree?"
"Nature does everything now," I replied; "It used to be the Lord; but it is Nature now. In a few years more, it will be Science. When we tire of that, it will be Accident. And after that, Something even nobler."
"But the tree will still be a tree," she answered gently. . . . (II, 263)

In a world of competing theories and confusion about the why of things, there was comfort in her answer. For Blackmore, a tree itself was a refuge, a living fact amidst uncertainties as he kept returning in imagination to the pastoral landscapes of pre-Darwinian nature.

Nostalgia is the keynote of *Christowell*, the first of his im-aginative retreats from the troubled air of the 1880s. The title names a fictitious village, perhaps based on Christow, but farther from Exeter and much higher on Dartmoor. The action begins on a sunny April morning "forty years ago" when even the weather was better, and it continues through a springtime of barely interrupted pastoralism for over 100 pages. The stock pastoral figures are here: a mysterious gentleman, "Captain Larks," in retreat from the wars and scandals of the great world; his daughter Rose, and her well-born lover, who finds life transformed by her presence: "It is like coming out of the shade into the light, from the winter to the summer, from a coal mine to a meadow full of bright flowers, and sunshine."[14] They live in a world that sometimes seems, like themselves, too good to be true.

Fortunately, these figures of pastoral romance are offset by their comic counterparts. The upstart family of Sir Joseph Touchwood, a businessman with a gaudy new estate, take part in a social comedy, along with the spunky bachelor parson, Mr. Short; and the cast includes a number of Dartmoor rustics. Of these, Pugsley the carrier is the most articulate and knowledgeable, his business making him the connecting link between Exeter and the little hamlets on the moor. As a spokesman for rustic views, he matches wits with Parson Short near the start of the novel, after an accident upon the road. Pugsley's calm acceptance of his predicament affronts the parson, who finds him at ease by the roadside, feeding himself and his horse, with one cart-wheel stuck in a hole and broken pots littering the ground. "All men is clay," as he says, but Parson Short has no time for reflection:

"How now, Pugsley? Stuck fast like this, and the captain's pots smashed up like that!" . . .
"Stuck slow, I karls it, Passon Shart. And thicky cloam be smashed, more down than oop. If her baided oop, her wud 'a been all zound." (15 - 16)

The lugubrious word-play follows the vein of William Barnes in "The Waggon a-stooded," where a cynical rustic keeps correcting his companion:

> *GEORGE*
> Well, here we be, then, wi' the vu'st poor lwoad
> O' vuzz we brought, a-stooded in the road.
> *JEAMES*
> The road, George, no. There's na'r a road. That's wrong.
> If we'd a road, we mid ha' got along.
> *GEORGE*
> Noo road! Ees 'tis, the road that we do goo.
> *JEAMES*
> Do goo, George, no. The pleãce we can't get drough. [15]

This kind of wit may try some readers' patience, and in the novel it certainly annoys Parson Short. But it is authentic West Country humor, noted by Henry Williamson in Devon in the 1920s. [16] At the start of *Christowell*, it establishes a difference between two classes of characters, those with Pugsley's "large resignation" to accidents and those with Short's educated impatience: "If your time is worthless, mine is not." The parson will never learn Pugsley's art of making time go slow enough to be enjoyed.

The mingling of rustic views with those of their social betters is one charm of the novel. The contrast continues when the heroine visits Moretonhampstead, the site of a special wonder, the "dancing tree" that provides the stage for a scene worthy of the early Hardy. The broad limbs support a platform for dancing on the evening of May Day, while three fiddlers play from their perches in the branches, and lanternlight and moonlight shine through "innumerable buds" upon the circling couples. As in Hardy, they dance to time's music, with past years present in "the rugged lines of heartwood, scarred with the jocosities of bygone dancers; whose names were wearing out, upon the tombstones down below" (108). The richness of the scene is evoked from multiple viewpoints. While the narrator reflects on time, the refined heroine watches from an upstairs window, wondering if the platform is a "fit place for ladies." At her side, Pugsley, the local authority on decorum, assures her that "If any man offendeth, in zider, ale, or langowich . . . us kicketh 'un out o' the tree, wi' out no rasoning, and a' cometh down zober, on the backside of his head. Never has no call to do it twice, Miss" (103). The rustic viewpoint again qualifies the heroine's genteel one after she commends the dancers' courtesy: "Why, they bow to one another continually!" This time Mrs. Pugsley sets her straight: "Not they, Miss; never a one of them. 'Tis the branches makes them duck their heads, for fear of an orkard clout on 'em. Good manners coom'th convanient so" (108).

The scene stays more distant than it would in Hardy, for the heroine never joins the dancers, and the chapter ends with two heroic acts which start her romance with Jack Westcombe. Rustic and genteel youth have separate ways of meeting in the stratified society that Blackmore represents. Yet the time for each meeting is the same, the May Day night of an old fertility celebration, seen here as the Dartmoor version of the Roman "festival of Pales" (102) that was held to insure the fruitful increase of flocks and herds. By bringing the young of both classes together on this occasion, the story shows their common part in the order of nature. However genteel a couple may be, their lives are fed by the land and timed by the seasons. This fact underlies a later contrast when a romantic idyll at sunset precedes a sweaty harvest chapter, and the lovers' concern with flowers and promises gives way to Sam Slowbury's desire for cider and a spot in the shade. Representing opposite extremes of sentiment and realism, both scenes fall within the pastoral tradition, and together give a balanced picture of man's place in the natural world.

Behind the pastoral shrubbery grinds the heavy machinery of a melodramatic plot. Unlike the principal characters in *Mary Anerley*, the young lover, the heroine, and her father are too virtuous to cause any troublesome action; that responsibility is left to a particularly malignant, fiery-faced villain who brings the wiles of London and the brute power of Dartmoor to bear upon Captain Larks in his pastoral retreat. In scenes at night on the moor, the villain schemes with his henchman, Black Wenlow, to destroy the captain (a nobleman's missing heir) and he toys with the idea of abducting the heroine, that feat being almost obligatory in melodrama. The pastoral idyll is as vulnerable as Captain Larks when he sits among his ripening grapes, smoking his pipe, while Wenlow from the shadows levels his sights at the gardener's chest and prepares to squeeze the trigger (349). But this outlaw is far less bloodthirsty than Carver Doone and by no means is the devil who "lives on Dartmoor" (99). The villain, George Gaston, very nearly is; but his henchman, like the hulking Sam Slowbury, merely embodies a natural force that comes under the temporary control of evil.

Evil keeps darkening the story as the summer passes. The present troubles stem from a betrayal and a consequent wave of panic years before in the Peninsular Campaign; that past episode shows how nature when violated can recoil upon the nerves of a guilty man. Another and more flamboyant act of nature comes at the climax of the novel, when disaster strikes the center of a community, the Christowell church, where the congregation and the villain have gathered on a stifling late-summer afternoon. Inspired by accounts of the great storm that hit the high-towered church at Widecombe-in-the-Moor on 21 October 1638, this spectacular scene has ambiguous implications. These come directly from Blackmore's seventeenth-century sources, which represent the storm as a manifestation of divine power and judgment while leaving room for the idea that it is the immediate production of the devil. The writer of "A True Relation" of the disaster at Widecombe reminded his audience of Divine Omnipotence: "*Hee causeth the vapours to ascend from the ends of the earth, and maketh lightnings for the raine, and bringeth the winde out of the treasures of the earth, so unsearchable is his Wisedome, and his waies past finding out.*" (Psalm 135:7; Romans 11:33).[17] Yet the devil might be allowed to work upon the parish as he worked upon Job, according to a latter commentator who insisted that "such dreadful thunders and lightnings don't arise by chance or the meer motion of matter."[18] Whatever the immediate cause, the ultimate power over the effect

is God's, according to all the accounts and these verses by a sur-
vivor: "Light out of Darkness, sweet out of bitter root,/Heaven out
of hell, who but the Lord can do't?"[19]

The novel quietly presents the theological implications while
forcefully reproducing the details from the contemporary accounts.
The seventeenth-century reports supply the imagery—the darkness
and the stench inside the church before the thunderbolt, the eight
boys piled unharmed in a heap inside the communion rails, the dog
taken up in the air and whirled three times around (seven times in
the novel) before falling dead on the floor, and the grotesque death
of the warriner, whose "head was cloven, his skull rent into three
peeces, and his braines throwne upon the ground whole."[20]
Blackmore let the warriner escape and transferred his fate to George
Gaston, the villain, whose "brains were gone, and lay behind him in
a grey heap on the flags" (390). Like the man at Widecombe,
Gaston is found in the pew, leaning upon his elbow, but his hand
clutches the heroine's skirt in a frozen gesture of fear and perhaps
penitence.

His pitiful last seconds of life do nothing to simplify the func-
tion of the storm. If the lightning were punitive, in spite of his
changing heart, it would not be simply the villain's just reward, for
other characters are killed or burnt by it. Having heard the
minister's text—"Let me fall into the hand of the Lord" (387)—the
people first act as if Judgment Day is upon them. Never guessing
that the fireball was aimed at Mr. Gaston, they decide afterwards
that it was the "roaring fury of the Evil One" (392), come to claim
the soul of an impious blacksmith. This newly made legend saves
everyone from "thinking ill of the House of the Lord" or of
themselves, since the slain blacksmith brought on the Satanic fury.
Blackmore leaves the storm open to interpretation, but the rustics
see it as demonic, a crowning display of the devil's fireworks after
Sam Slowbury's report of them early in the story (115). To Sam, evil
is the main actor, as it may seem to be in a novel which sets both
"defiance" and "heroism" beneath the pastoral virtues of
"patience, cheerfulness, and modesty, truth, simplicity, and loving-
kindness" (410). But no matter where or why the lightning strikes,
these virtues perform their own quiet action in *Christowell* while
grand schemes and passions burn to ashes.

II   *The Community under Attack in* Springhaven

A sense of invading evil is still more immediate in Blackmore's most ambitious historical novel, *Springhaven: A Tale of the Great War* (1887), timed for the patriotic celebrations of Queen Victoria's Golden Jubilee. "The Great War," of course, refers not to the one on the way but to the struggle with Napoleon, a conflict that often comes into Blackmore's fiction. This time it pervades a whole novel, set mainly in a once-quiet fishing village on the Sussex coast.[21] With the French threatening from across the Channel and traitors lurking in the neighborhood, the story breathes an atmosphere of paranoia. The omniscient narrator himself seems infected by it, though his immediate enemies are not the Free-thinkers of the French Revolution but the Radicals and Gladstonian Liberals of Blackmore's own decade. Contrasting the heroic militance of 1802 - 1805 with the compromising policies of Gladstone, the narrator clutters the story with petulant asides which one hostile reviewer dismissed as "eternal political humbug."[22] Passages like the following suggest an ill-tempered Tory tract for the times: "Britannia now is always in the wrong, in the opinion of her wisest sons, if she dares to defend herself against weak enemies; what then would her crime be if she buckled her corslet against the world! To prostitute their mother is the philanthropy of Communists."[23] These grumblings create strange discords with Blackmore's normally genial tone, as if his humor were still tainted by the satiric spleen of *Thomas Upmore*. Where the narrator's tone does not make the novel distressing, the polite conversations of admirals and young ladies often make it tedious, while characters ranging from fishermen to Lord Nelson, Napoleon, and George III threaten to stretch the plot completely out of shape. The multitude is enough to make one wish for the simpler design of Hardy's earlier novel of the Napoleonic era, *The Trumpet-Major* (1880). But if literature has room for the patriotic novel, *Springhaven* with all its faults is a credit to its kind and worthy of its place in the Everyman's Library. An English critic once called it "the greatest historical novel of its generation."[24]

The book's strength lies first of all in its portrayal of the "middling people of Springhaven" who form a microcosm of England in a time of crisis.[25] The villagers have their own structure of authority under their "headman," Zebedee Tugwell, the captain of the fishing fleet. But independent as they are, they exist within a larger structure represented by the vicar, the bellicose Rev. Twemlow; the chief landlord, Admiral Darling; and King George himself, who comes to review his troops on the Downs above the village. The novel shows how the great national events reverberate down the chain of authority into the lives of the little people, where abstractions and decisions must be dealt with concretely. The process begins with the report of the king's speech from the throne in November 1802 calling for preparations to renew the war with France. In Springhaven, Parson Twemlow responds with a fire-eating sermon in which he accuses the villagers of caring more for their "flesh-pots and fish-kettles" than for their native land. "And he said that they would wake up some day and find themselves turned into Frenchmen, for all things were possible with the Lord. . . . the abomination of desolation would be set up over their doorways, and the scarlet woman of Babylon would revel in their sanctuaries" (50). Thus clothed in biblical symbols, the news from the great world comes home to the fishermen, who discuss it after church at the pub. There Captain Tugwell warns against hasty action and neutralizes the sermon by referring to local personalities: "My opinion is that Parson Twemlow were touched up by his own conscience for having a nephew more French than English . . ." (50). Despite the rhetoric from throne and pulpit, the village deals with the French threat in the concrete terms of anecdote and gossip. It will have no stronger reality for them until warships do battle off their coast.

With a whole scale of characters to be affected by each event, the novel has a further strength in the way it distributes error and evil among them, instead of leaving all the bad with the half-French villain, Caryl Carne. A master of seduction, Carne has a mistress, but so does England's greatest national hero, and Mrs. Twemlow will not let her husband risk his career by preaching a word against fornication in Nelson's presence: "Lord Nelson won't know it; he is too simple-minded. But Admiral Darling will never forgive us for insulting him while he is staying at the Hall" (12). Admiral Darling's own daughter, Dolly, is the most flawed of Blackmore's heroines; and by falling in love with Carne she becomes indirectly responsible for her father's death. Being both clever and foolish, she can throw the novel's apparent values in a doubtful light. In a book that often sounds like a glorification of war, the first sign of her flaw is her boredom with "dull peace" and her desire for the excitement of battle (4 - 5). Restlessness aligns her with the villain, yet her father also yearns for war, claiming that it "encourages the best men of the day" and "brings out the difference between right and wrong, which are quite smothered up in peace time" (47). If the admiral's words are supposed to express wisdom, they are undercut finally by the professional motives behind his speech: "And what is the use of a noble fleet, unless it can get some fighting?" Because this good man's views sound so much like his restless daughter's, they qualify the militant patriotism of the novel.

More complexity comes through Dolly's candid speech to the villain about the ideals of the French Revolution. Much as Blackmore hated revolution and the spell of political abstractions, he lets his selfish heroine express his own attitude: "I am an English girl, and I care very little for things that I don't see—such as justice, liberty, rights of people, and all that" (309). Her pragmatism is Blackmore's—made to sound less cold when she goes on to name specific persons whom she does care for. But her self-centered character heightens the selfish ring of the speech and may make the villain's radical idealism seem a preferable alternative. For intentionally or not, Blackmore has already created sympathy for the radical viewpoint by depicting one brutal English reaction against it. When Zebedee Tugwell flogs his grown son, Dan, for radical tendencies, the authoritarian structure of a traditional society is laid open for questioning.

The fisherman's son commits two crimes against the traditions of Springhaven. First, he nurses a "hopeless love" (76) for Dolly, his playmate in the years of childhood when the caste system could be overlooked. His presumption affronts the admiral's housekeeper, though the gardener, "whose views were loose and liberal," trusts to "Natur' " instead of caste: "Dan'el is a brave boy, and might fight his way to glory, and then they has the pick of the femmels up to a thousand pound a year" (23). Dolly herself admires the young man enough to complain of what a "fearful shame it is . . . that he should be nothing but a fisherman" (43). Yet their romance gets nowhere, and Dan will find no one of his own caste to marry by the time the novel ends. His fancy for Dolly makes him a malcontent, unable to feel at home in the rank of his birth. His restlessness leads to an overt crime against authority. Defying his father's wishes, he joins the radical "Fair, Free and Frisky Club" to discuss Justice, Liberty, and the Rights of Man. Against these hated abstractions, Captain Tugwell has one weapon—a whip for the back of his twenty-year-old son, "a grown man," as his wife points out, "a'most

as big as yourself, and a good half-head taller! Suppose he was to hit
you back again!" The father answers, "If he did, I should just kill
him . . ." (161).

The conflict of fathers and sons in Blackmore now breaks into the
open, with Zebedee and Dan representing two sides of their
author's nature—stubborn conservatism and stubborn in-
dependence. In earlier novels, the greater fault rests with the
domineering father; now, the father is more overbearing than ever,
but his views sound far closer than Dan's to Blackmore's Tory con-
victions. Zebedee accuses his son of trying to "upset all the State,
the King, the House of Lords, and the Parliamentary House, and all
as is descended from the Romans," while Dan asserts his right to
take part in free discussion:

"You know, father, that the world goes on by reason, and justice, and good-
will, and fair play—"
"No, it don't," cried the captain, who had found what he wanted; "if it
had to wait for they, it would never go on at all. It goes on by government,
and management, and discipline, and the stopping of younkers from their
blessed foolery, and by the ten commandments, and the proverbs of King
Solomon. You to teach your father how the world goes on! Off with your
coat, and I'll teach you." (168)

By flogging his son, Zebedee asserts the rule of the old system, but
the punishment drives Dan from the house and makes the system
look unworthy of defending.

The two rebellious children, Dan and Dolly, stand near the center of the action. Both fall victim to the villain's seductions, and
both must be rescued if the story is to end with Blackmore's usual
motif of regeneration. For Dan, new life is supposed to come
through a baptism of blood at Trafalgar, where he helps to care for
the dying national hero. Dolly's rebirth is less stylized and more difficult, for by trusting Caryl Carne she helps him kill her father and
then suffers from a despairing sense of guilt. Only the resource of a
faithful neglected lover saves her from suicide. The community
itself is saved through the villain's death and the sacrifice at
Trafalgar, two signs of the providence that Blackmore and Parson
Twemlow saw working in history. The novel ends with a New Year
that looks both ways—toward new life in the celebration of
marriage, and toward sacrificial death, commemorated in "the
grand funeral of the hero," Lord Nelson.

Springhaven is rich in the characterization of individuals and the
community, but many critics doubted Blackmore's artistry in shap-
ing the story. The plot seemed to lack "one main thread: it has
many threads which are not properly interwoven, but dangle loosely
about, and the absence of a well-marked design, to which all else in
the pattern is subordinate, distracts and fatigues the attention. . . ."[26] Gerard Manley Hopkins found the same weakness.
Though still a "devoted admirer" of Blackmore's "wordpainting,"
he now felt disillusioned with the novelist whom he once praised in
the same breath with Thomas Hardy. He called the "construction"
of *Springhaven* clumsy, the "character drawing superficial and
sometimes melodramatic."[27] These charges are hard to refute, unless the community itself is accepted as the center of the novel.
Then individual characterization will appear subordinate to the portrayal of the whole village, and even the strokes of melodrama may
be seen as ways to represent extremes of good and evil inside a
microcosmic setting. The villain, however, is a fuller character than
Hopkins realized, for the young man is a study in alienation.
Estranged not only from his father's land but also from his own existence, Carne never quite forgives the world for "producing" him
(90). Lacking roots of his own, he strikes against the traditional
loyalties that give anyone else a sense of community. His accidental
self-destruction is not only a flashy stroke of melodrama but also the
sort of end that his character has been driving toward all along.

Hopkins voiced another complaint which is harder to deal with.
"There is," he wrote, "a vein of stupid jocularity all about 'nose'
and 'stomach' and 'breeches' and 'fine feeding' which downright
disgusts me." Apparently he took offense at the description of Lord
Nelson, a skinny man whose waistcoat came "over the place where
his stomach should have been" but whose "white plush breeches"
were made before the months of peace had "fattened him a little,"
causing a tight fit (11). If this disgusted Hopkins, he was sure to
find more indelicacies further on, as when Mrs. Tugwell reminds
her son of his infancy: "you used to lie here in the hollow of my
arm, without a stitch of clothes on, and kind people was tempted to
smack you in pleasure, because you did stick out so prettily" (163).
But these passages could only offend Victorian squeamishness or induce weariness with a certain vein of humor; modern readers would
be far more likely to feel affronted by the narrator's politics.

Still, Hopkins has a point, for something is offensive about the narrator's comic sensibility. Perhaps the clearest sign of it is a jocose remark in his account of the bloodshed at Trafalgar: an "eager-minded Frenchman . . . must have been off his head; and his inductive process was soon amended by the logic of facts, for his head was off him" (425). In that unfunny, inappropriate word-play, Blackmore reveals a basic limitation, a lack of tact when his sympathies fall short of his subject. Without describing a battle, Hardy could evoke a deeper sense of war in *The Trumpet-Major*, when Nelson's "great silent ship, with her population of blue-jackets, marines, officers, captain, and the admiral who was not to return alive, passed like a phantom" off Portland Bill (Chap. XXXIV). At the end of Hardy's novel, the trumpet-major marches "into the night" toward final silence on a Spanish battlefield; in Blackmore's, the carnage on board the *Victory* becomes a display of fancy sharpshooting. The difference in sensitivity to suffering, not Blackmore's attention to breeches and stomachs, is one reason for agreeing with Hopkins that as a novelist, "Hardy is a finer man."[28]

CHAPTER 6

Pastoral Realism in Perlycross

I have taken the romancer's liberty with his raw materials. [1]

I N his last three novels, Blackmore dealt with a more immediate source of pain than the historic naval battle which had
inspired a flashy chapter in *Springhaven*. When Lucy Blackmore
died in January 1888, he felt the deepest grief he had ever known.
"I am cast into the wilderness at sixty-two," he told his publisher;
"All the spring of my mind seems gone. . . . I cannot write. . .the
pleasure of gardening is gone."[2] He soon wrote again, but *Kit and
Kitty* (1889), *Perlycross* (1894), and *Dariel* (1897) all reflect the pain
of losing the dearest person in his life. They echo his loss by depicting the loneliness of widowers or the ordeal of a man whose wife
mysteriously disappears. This ordeal became the subject of a story
begun in the autumn following Mrs. Blackmore's death. Set in the
Thames valley near Sunbury at the time when the Blackmores moved into Gomer House, *Kit and Kitty* reads like an attempt through
fantasy to bring back the lost springtime of their marriage. In the
face of death, Blackmore views experience with "the eye of imagination" and reconstructs it as what a defender of romantic fiction, Hall Caine, would call a "beautiful lie," at once "false to fact"
and "true to faith."[3] In this instance, the fiction is true to his faith
that his loss need not be eternal.

The author enters the story by dividing himself into two
characters, Kit Orchardson, the young romantic narrator, and his
crusty bachelor uncle, Cornelius. This elderly market-gardener
represents Blackmore's present workaday self—the grumbling
taskmaster who takes a "glass of hot rum and water" every Saturday
night "to restore himself after paying wages."[4] Each character en-
dures the loss of a beloved woman. As a youth, Uncle Cornelius lost
his sweetheart, a servant, through the vicious irresponsibility of the
local gentry, who are portrayed with none of the indulgence or es-
teem that might be expected of a Tory novelist. With his uncle's sad

experience in the background, Kit marries and begins a pastoral life in an orchard cottage before his wife vanishes with their money. The young husband must pass the test of trusting her, "his better self" (456), despite his neighbors' cynicism and long nights alone in the kitchen, away from the marriage bed which he refuses to sleep in until she returns.

She does return to him, first in a dream and then as another Persephone or Alcestis in Blackmore's myths of loss and recovery. But their meeting in the orchard has a grisly parallel near the climax of the story in the reunion of an aristocratic man and wife. A long-absent rogue comes back to England as a leper and demands that his proud wife embrace him. The violent end of this family ruined the romance with the shock of melodrama, according to the *Spectator*;[5] for later readers, the love scenes themselves might be a worse annoyance. Whatever is the matter, the story lacks the humor and descriptive power that go with a similar plot in *Cripps, the Carrier*. This time the reliance upon myth seems too easy a solution to loneliness and grief. The bride's return makes the grieving look misplaced, even if the event is simply Blackmore's way of representing on earth the restoration of life that faith hopes for in eternity. According to Hall Caine in 1890, the artist has the right to overstep earthly limits, for imagination is "the eye of faith" that looks through the "enormous preponderance of evil" in this world, sees the triumph of good in the world to come, and can shape its vision in narratives with happy endings.[6] The theory deserves consideration, but Blackmore might have been wiser to accept the limited viewpoint expressed by an old Devonshire cook upon hearing that the love-sick hero has died in a snowdrift: "No more courtin' for Measter Kit in this laife. A' may do what a' wool in kingdom coom" (154).

For his next-to-last and possibly his next-to-best novel, Blackmore turned from romantic myth to the earthly realities of a parish in East Devon, where the kingdom, if coming, moves at a snail's pace through one rural year. *Perlycross: A Tale of the Western Hills* explores the errors of mortal vision in a fearful little world which has forgotten how to be a community. Like *Kit and Kitty*, the book deals with loss but without straining to suggest paradise regained. Nor is there any fireball or pistol flash to resolve the question of evil. The kindly squire who is ill at the outset cannot be cured; the sad parson never learns how his wife fell to her death, though a poacher tells him the devil had a hand in it, and a witchlike old woman promises an explanation. As if under an evil spell, the village church seems in danger of falling. The parson's task is to restore the building and preserve a center for the community that it was meant to serve.

This quest generates the plot. It is complicated after the squire's funeral by an apparent grave-robbery which sends the parish on a winterlong hunt for a villian. But for almost the only time in Blackmore's novels, no villain emerges. Instead, *Perlycross* represents the fear, the silliness, and the pain that go into the making of scapegoats. One victim's suffering is recalled in the title and made explicit when the squire's Spanish widow gazes at the image of the "Tortured One" upon her ivory crucifix. Before this figure, her feelings change from outrage to sorrow in a scene that foreshadows the larger movement in the life of the parish. "Love will drive the anger out,"[7] says the village schoolmaster. Driving anger out of a community completes the action of a pastoral that ends in spring with the final shape of comedy. But the process is more earthy than romantic, and it occurs in a world that owes less to the author's mythic imagination than to his memories of a boyhood home.

I *Culmstock and "Perlycross"*

Blackmore's memories for this novel went back almost sixty years to the summer of 1835 when his father began serving as curate of All Saints Church in Culmstock, a village on the River Culm east of Tiverton. The clear stream with its "stickles" of swift water had stayed alive in his imagination as the scene of "Crocker's Hole" (1879), his fine fishing-story about helping one of his father's pupils land a mighty trout in a night-cap. The pupil, "John Pike," awes little Richard in the story and returns as the "young prince" of fishermen in *Perlycross*. In 1890, Blackmore's Culmstock days came back to him in a letter from an old schoolmate who recalled "pugilistic encounters between green aphids" under the microscope in the curate's study, "the dainty glistening of very fine champagne currants in the rectory garden," and the "interruption of our own juvenile sports by the incursion and horse-play of loutish village hobba-de-hoys."[8] Within a year, the novel must have begun taking shape, for by March 1892 Blackmore was bargaining over the serialization of "Perly Cross." He finished it by 12 September 1893, three months after the installments started appearing in *Macmillan's* (June 1893 - July 1894).

Almost immediately, natives of the Culm Valley recognized their village. The fictional curate, Parson Penniloe, and the schoolmaster of Perlycross, Sergeant Jakes, were identified with the Rev. John Blackmore and William Jacobs; other characters suggested more people of the neighborhood, and the setting brought to mind a familiar landscape. Writing to the *Critic* from San Antonio in 1894, William Corner found the "manners, customs, superstitions, prejudices" of *Perlycross* all true to life; the whole book, he said, "reads like a long letter from home. . . ."[9] The schoolmaster's grandson, Edwin Jacobs, wrote Blackmore from London that his "description of the little Devonshire village, in almost every particular, so closely resembles the one in which I first saw the light, and some of the characters are so clearly portrayed, that it is either a marvellous coincidence, or it must be one and the same place." Seeing both his father and his grandfather in the schoolmaster, Jacobs especially marveled at a bit of family history that found its way into the novel. Like the fictional schoolmaster, his father had been rejected by the inkeeper's daughter, a Miss Haddon, who married Mr. Jacobs's brother, a butcher, instead, "But how you could possibly have known that, entirely passes my comprehension. . . ."[10]

Having offended a family at Oare with his portrait of Farmer Snowe in *Lorna Doone*, Blackmore responded with mingled gratitude and uneasiness. "I have taken the romancer's liberty with his raw materials," he wrote to Edwin Jacobs, adding, "it would grieve me very greatly to find that my vague portraits have caused pain to any one connected with the originals." In his public reply to William Corner, he maintained that only the schoolmaster and the curate represented specific persons from Culmstock, and he closed with an observation meant to discourage further source-hunting: "Being only ten-twelve years old then, and far away at school for most of the year, I must have been endowed with a wonderful memory and very quick powers of perception, if I could present any picture of the natives, even half as true as Mr. Corner has kindly imagined."[11] But the evidence points toward a wonderfully observant and retentive mind, while a writer who knew him well belived that he "invented very little" and depended "largely on fact and memory."[12]

What Blackmore remembered was first of all a landscape, a pastoral valley between two arms of the Blackdown Hills. Long after 1835, its sheltered remoteness justified the local saying, "Out of the world into Culmstock."[13] The parish was once a world of its own, centered in the village beside the little river. Along the road up the slope from the stone bridge stood several shops and many cob-walled cottages, mostly without gardens but white-washed after the cholera scare of 1832 (mentioned in the novel), when they were provided at last with casement windows.[14] High above the cluster of thatched roofs, the gray church tower held the amazing yew tree, springing then as now from the battlements. Northward across the river, the new woollen mill stood at the foot of a green hillside, while around the lower end of the village apple orchards came up to the road and the last cottage walls. Beyond the trees were hedged fields and pastures, with some newly enclosed plots for the industrious poor to rent and cultivate on land belonging to the Dean and Chapter of Exeter Cathedral. Above the fields were the Blackdowns, stopping abruptly to the south at the wooded bank of Hackpen Hill and to the north at the flint-strewn slope of bracken and furze below Culmstock Beacon.

In Blackmore's childhood, the only sounds to reach the parish from the great world came from the coachman's horn on the road from Tiverton to Wellington. Exeter was then a far-off city; its stone-masons are considered "foreign" in the novel, where even the natives of adjoining parishes are looked upon with suspicion. Roads through the valley ran between hedgerows so overgrown with brambles, bushes, and small trees that in summer the sunken lanes became leafy tunnels, barely wide enough for the pack-horses carrying goods to and from the village.[15] An old man living in 1900 claimed to remember the "first wagon and the first spring-cart" in Culmstock; in his youth, ploughs were still drawn by oxen, prompted by the ploughboy's goad and chanted song: "Up along, jump along, Pretty, Spark, and Tender." In the farmhouse at night, the apprenticed boy might eat his potatoes, salt pork, and black barley bread from a hollow carved in his master's table, after pudding and treacle were served first "to lessen the appetite."[16] He belonged to a rural order that had gone on for centuries and would end only in Blackmore's lifetime.

The curate's son would have dined differently in the parsonage. He grew up with no experience of the ploughboy's toil, and he recorded nothing of it in the novel. But in the curious years between ten and sixteen, while his father lived at Culmstock, he was bound to learn something about the rougher side of parish life. Smugglers bringing lace and brandy from the southern coast appear in *Perlycross*, along with allusions to the sheep-stealing that made the place notorious. The last man to be hanged for this crime in Devon was from the parish, and local historians still warn against saying " 'Baa' to a Culmstock man."[17] The rowdiness of the country fair, with wrestling matches and brawling, forms the comic climax of the novel, while another lively, pugnacious scene depicts the beating of the parish bounds. Led by the earnest curate in *Perlycross*, this noisy ritual maintained the parish frontiers and sometimes led to open warfare with rival bands from Uffculme and Hemyock. The custom stopped after a brawl between the marching parishioners and a railway gang who raided their cartload of cider.[18]

But during the 1830s Culmstock suffered from less picturesque troubles which are almost entirely missing from the novel. These grew out of poverty and unemployment once the new factories in the north had deprived most of the cottage weavers of their occupation. The woollen mill did little to relieve the general distress in a parish of nearly 1,500 people. Neither a system of "out-of-door" relief, which kept many families outside the poor-house, nor a scheme to provide food and work by renting quarter-acre plots to the poor at five shillings annually could stop the drift of people away from the parish, which lost half its population by 1900.[19]

Nor could these measures stop the spread of bitterness and distrust once the farm-workers of neighboring counties broke into open revolt in 1830. When John Blackmore arrived in 1835, a new scheme for handling the problem stirred fresh anger among the paupers of Culmstock. A plan to build a workhouse at Maidendown frightened them with the prospect of forced labor to replace the out-door relief that allowed them to live in in their drab cottages. One of their leaders sent the vestry chairman, Mr. Thomas Short, an unsigned warning against building a "Poor Man's Prison": "you need not Put yourself to that Expense for if you do we shall have the Trouble of Pulling it Down again. . . .Dost thee think Poor men will stand quietly to be made slaves. . . ."[20] The note ends with a threat to paint Mr. Short's "white heart Reed" (*sic*) with his "own blood." Earlier, a similar threat, accompanied by a "cat's head stuck through with a knife," supposedly went to Major Octavious Temple, the father of Blackmore's schoolmate, the future Archbishop of Canterbury. Sometime before leaving Culmstock in 1834, Temple was pelted with sod from the churchyard after farmers persuaded their laborers that his support for a candidate who opposed the Corn Laws (which protected the price of home-grown grain) could cost them their jobs.[21]

None of these events goes into the novel, even though Blackmore must have learned something about them while boarding at Tiverton with the sons of Major Temple. The poaching, smuggling, and sheep-stealing in *Perlycross* appear as individual exploits, not as signs of smoldering rebellion. "Every one" in the fictional parish loves the largest landowner, Sir Thomas Waldron (37); and the only open revolt against the "ceremonial regime"[22] of parson and squire occurs on Shrove Tuesday when a gang of roughs start to thrash the curate. But their anger stems from his plan to abolish the Perlycross Fair; nothing is said of their poverty. The desperation that could break out in such violence was one of the "raw materials" from Culmstock which Blackmore never grasped, or took the "romancer's liberty" of ignoring.

This omission needs to be acknowledged before endorsing the claim that *Perlycross* is "one of the best pastoral novels in our language."[23] For the term *pastoral*, long suspect, has become nearly synonymous with evasion and distortion. Under the influence of the Marxist critic Raymond Williams, two editors have dismissed the "pastoral vision" as a way of obscuring the "harshness of actual social and economic organization" in rural England.[24] As a nostalgic Tory, Blackmore is vulnerable to the charge, and his fiction generally gives favorable pictures of country squires and their traditional allies, the Anglican clergy. But glimpses of rural poverty occur in several novels, and if he ignores the specific problems in Culmstock, he does acknowledge the unrest that swept southern England in the 1830s. In *Perlycross*, the dying Squire Waldron alludes to the farm-laborers' revolt and strikes a penitent note even as he denounces the agitation for reform. "I think . . . that we don't behave half well enough to those who do all the work for us," he tells the parson. "And I am quite sure that we Tories feel it, ay and try to better it, ten times as much as all those spouting radical reformers do." Oddly mingling self-reproach with self-justification, he thrusts the blame upon men who usually lacked a landowner's opportunity to exploit the workers. But when he asks, "Who is at the bottom of all these shocking riots, and rick-burnings?" the expected Tory answer is not forthcoming. The culprit is not the radical politician but the landlord or rich farmer who buys a threshing-machine—"the man who puts iron, and boiling water, to rob a poor fellow of his bread and bacon. You'll find none of that on any land of mine" (32).

Because rural poverty antedates the steam engine, his answer sounds simplistic, but in his decade it made sense to the laborers who smashed the new machines. Eventually thousands of workers would abandon the countryside, leaving the ploughing, hay-making, and harvest to a few men in tractors. Their exodus marked the end of the society that Squire Waldron values and that *Perlycross* represents. The squire's stand against mechanization may look Ruskinian and quixotic, but he has at least phrased the essential problem in terms that a Marxist could understand: "those who do all the work" have not received justice. Acknowledged in an early chapter, this fact underlies Blackmore's pastoral vision of society. To be a community, the parish depends upon charitable actions; it fails when a doctor says, "If a man could not pay for it, let him not be ill; or at any rate go to the workhouse, and be done for in the lump" (105); or when a son lets his aged parents live in the poorhouse and limits his charity to two ounces of tobacco for them each Wednesday (202). Without a benevolent squire, there would be no one "to help the struggling tradesman, to bury the aged cripple, to do any of those countless deeds of good-will and humanity, which are less than the discount of the interest of the debt, due from the wealthy to the poor" (54). Benevolence, in other words, is only a step toward justice. With its model squire, Perlycross is spared the economic distress of Culmstock and faced instead with the scandal of a reported grave-robbery, a different sort of trouble but still a threat to the communal life.

II   *The Pastoral of a Community on Trial*

Like Blackmore's earlier novels of community, *Perlycross* teems with characters who prevent the author from offering a simplistic "single view" of rural existence.[25] Though the narrator is omniscient, he does not tell all that he knows, and the point of view keeps shifting from one character to the next. As they meet to talk over or try a hand at solving the mystery of the missing coffin, the story unfolds in a series of framed pictures or "idylls" in the tradition of Blackmore's master, Theocritus. These scenes slowly create one large picture of both the community and the landscape, for each conversation is set at a key point in the valley: the churchyard gate, the squire's garden, Farmer Horner's potato field, the parson's kitchen. Representing almost every rank in the local hierarchy, the characters range from the gentry, the sporting vicar who comes to cheer up his poor curate, and the lawyers and doctors from the larger world, to the half-witted poacher and the ancient Mrs. Tremlett, who demands a shilling from the parson, even on her death bed, before consenting to hear a prayer. In the sheer number of memorable minor characters, *Perlycross* is an impressive novel, and all the more so because one small place can hold so many. They still can stir the admiration that George Saintsbury felt for an author who fills "a whole village, and almost a whole district, with live people."[26] They form the fictional community and keep offering fresh views of it while the landscape changes with the seasons before the reader's eyes.

But the book presents problems for anyone who expects a plot to move in a straightforward manner. The plot eddies around a non-event, a false report of a grave-robbery, which for one critic made the story "much ado about nothing."[27] That action is fine for comedy, however, and the scandal prompts the whole scale of characters to reveal themselves in the light of one common concern.[28] More than any individual, the community itself becomes the protagonist, divided and threatened by its fears and suspicions. Looking for a different focus, the *Athenaeum* found the book formless, a "jungle" of "interminable talk."[29] At worst, the talk is "monotonous and tame"[30] when elderly doctors and the parson meet, or blushingly sentimental in the few love scenes. But in talking, the characters shift the emphasis from events to personal reactions, often revealing more about themselves than the subject of their conversation. The baker's wife may have seen the devil knocking on the parson's door, but her report only makes certain that she was peeping over the shrubbery to observe a strange visitor; the blacksmith may have seen two grave-robbers on Halloween night, but he is more precise about the ale he had drunk to console himself after the squire's funeral, or about his fear on the frosty road home from the pub, and the stillness in the house after he climbed meekly into bed with his sleeping wife: "there was no sound. . .without it was a rat or two, and the children snoring in the inner room, and the baby breathing in the cradle to the other side of the bed, that was strapped on, to come at for nursing of her" (62). All these unasked-for details keep expanding a picture of communal relationships that becomes as intricate as the network of lanes and footpaths across the valley. A traveler may feel lost between the hedgerows, but all roads lead somewhere, even when they go in circles.

The forward movement in *Perlycross* is circular without being repetitious, and it follows two sets of guideposts to mark the slow progress. These are the same markers that order time and space in a rural parish. As a movement through time, the story follows the seasons and the holy days of the church year; as the exploration of a place, it recreates the spatial order of Culmstock, which depends upon the river and the focal point of the parish church. The seasonal movement begins with wheat ripening in the summer of 1835 and ends the following May with trout rising to the fly along the Perle. Death comes to the squire just before the first frost; the blacksmith tells of the grave-robbers on the morning of All Saints Day, when Farmer Horner is harvesting his potatoes. The idea of digging up a body like a potato horrifies everyone, destroying all thought of heavenly rest and upsetting the parish throughout the winter. The discord with the church year increases on Christmas morning when a wall of the sanctuary settles again and the people bolt from their pews, just as the curate's text—"On earth, peace"—names what the community has lost. No peace will return until after a brawl on Shrove Tuesday and a drinking party on Ash Wednesday. Harmony between holy day and event, and within the parish, comes with the solving of the mystery on St. David's Day (March 1). The time is right for a discovery, since in one story the saint at his baptism was a means for restoring sight to the blind.

With the holy days marking the movement from discord to harmony within the parish, the church building itself represents the focus of spatial order for the imagined landscape. On a bluff beside the Perle, it stands as the "fixed point" of interchange between the human and the divine.[31] Passing almost under its shadow, the river flows westward like the metaphoric stream of human life. These symbols were ready-made for the novelist at Culmstock, where the yew tree springing from the church tower suggests a meeting point of nature and grace. Blackmore added one other quiet symbol by placing an abbey's "ivied ruins" behind the "grey power" of the flint-walled church. The image could have come from the next parish, where a new church stands near the ruins of Dunkeswell Abbey, dissolved in 1538 and soon plundered by a greedy owner.[32] Though the ruins in the novel seem scarcely more than a stage prop, they mark an earlier profanation of a holy place and point to the threat facing the present sanctuary. In danger of falling, the church apparently suffers the desecration of a grave-robbery, as if it had lost the power to "protect even its own dead" (269). Without a church, Perlycross would be without a center; hence the curate's effort to restore the building is also a quest to restore the focus of communal life.

So long as the church seems profaned and falling, with "ghouls and fiends" (442) haunting the graveyard, the parish stays at the mercy of its strong tendencies toward paranoia. These break the community into suspicious groups that have nothing more in common than their fears and a desire to find a scapegoat. From the outset, they feed their fears with talk of criminals like Burke and Hare, who murdered to collect cadavers, while the schoolboys terrorize the curate's son with tales of "Spring-heel Jack," a flame-spitting highwayman, on his way to Perlycross churchyard with his "bloody heart and dark lantern" (14).[33] After the baker's wife reports a mysterious stranger, possibly the Evil One himself, at the rectory door, the atmosphere is ripe for the blacksmith's story of his ordeal on Halloween night after Squire Waldron's funeral. Routed from bed by a "thundering noise going through the house, like the roaring of a bull," he hears a masked giant threaten to fire his thatch if he fails to tend a lame horse. In spite of terror, the blacksmith steals a glimpse of what seems to be a dead man's shroud in the cart under a tarpaulin. His story and an overhasty examination of the squire's grave set the parish hunting for scapegoats. The prime suspects are a cocky young outsider from Somerset, Dr. Fox, and Lady Waldron, a Spanish Catholic and therefore a likely murderer of her husband. "You know all these foreigners, how pat they are with poison," says Fox's ill-named sister, Christie (126). As for Lady Waldron, she would have Fox dismembered in the marketplace (206).

According to the blacksmith, the devil was abroad on the night of his ordeal, and the resulting ill-will suggests that he was right. But Perlycross has a few educated rationalists to oppose the native respect for demonic powers. Dr. Fox and the retired Dr. Gronow, the village skeptic, work out a rational plan to capture the real grave robbers at the Perlycross Fair. At least one suspect will be lured there by the chance to wrestle; and once he is caught, Fox can clear his name against local suspicion and marry the squire's daughter. The blustery Shrove Tuesday of the fair brings the novel to a comic crescendo, when a winter of pent-up fury in the parish erupts and exhausts itself in brawling. The episode is beautifully prepared for, with lines of characters converging on the village, the detectives laying their trap, and the weather preparing a still more startling surprise. Nature has a human agent in the huge wrestler Harvey Tremlett, the masked man who terrified the blacksmith and by now has become the doctors' prime suspect. After saving the curate from a thrashing, he enacts the local fighting spirit through the disciplined violence of wrestling. Urging him on against the outsider from Cornwall, the men of Perlycross vent their frustrations without guessing that their new hero will be arrested as the cause of the local scandal.

Through wrestling, Tremlett releases more energies than his own. When he defeats the Cornish champion and the jubilant Devonshire men start pounding the "Carnies" under a makeshift canvas roof, nature breaks loose with a fury that dwarfs and mocks the human outburst: "The great pole of red pine, fit mast for an Admiral, bearing all the structure overhead, snapped like a carrot, to a vast wild blast. In a weltering squash lay victor and vanquished, man with his fists up, and man eager to go at him. . . . Prostrate all, with mouths full of tallow, sawdust, pitch, and another fellow's toes. Many were for a twelvemonth limpers; but nobody went to Churchyard" (362 - 63). For those men still in action, the plot to arrest Tremlett leads only to more hard blows and the comic anticlimax of his trial for grave-robbery. Being a smuggler and not a resurrection man, he celebrates his innocence with a drinking party on the penitential day of Ash Wednesday. Doctor Fox's fine detective work has led nowhere.

But the storm and the fighting have brought about a catharsis of anger that leaves the parish ready for a new start. The scene of renewal on St. David's Day has just the right blend of humor and seriousness. The squire's rather loutish son has returned at last from the sea, and he waits on the churchyard wall while Penniloe baptizes a child named "Billy Jack." By accident, the new squire goes through an initiation of his own, making a sudden descent underground, if not to the underworld, where he discovers the missing coffin. He does not bring his father back from the dead, as he did in his sister's dream (221), but he comes up from the earth as a more worthy representative of the old squire. In practical terms, the change means that he will allow his sister to marry Dr. Fox and that he will pay for the final restoration of Perlycross Church. Through his generosity, the longtime loser, Parson Penniloe, wins his quest and emerges as a modest hero.

But all along Penniloe has filled an unsung hero's role by serving the community. Preaching, advising, visiting the sick, leading the parish in worship and ceremony, he comes close to the ideal that George Herbert set for himself in *The Country Parson*. Blackmore's portrayal of such faithful good will suggests an imaginative act of atonement with his father, the model for Penniloe. John Blackmore had been a conscientious priest at Culmstock, helping to complete the restoration of the church and to recover the stone screen that now stands beneath the east window.[34] Having known his father only from a distance, the novelist often wrote of estrangements between fathers and sons, and he may have identified with the youth in *Cradock Nowell* for whom " 'the governor' long had been the strangest of all puzzles."[35] Now, in representing the governor as Penniloe, he brought an image of his father back from the dead with sympathetic understanding.

The curate presides over the fishing idyll that ends the novel. From the riverbank where "the Priestwell brook glides in," he enjoys the May morning and wishes for a "homely rod such as St. Peter might have swung," while Dr. Gronow casts awkwardly for trout. These two contrasting men, one faithful and self-effacing, the other skeptical and a bit conceited, are joined by the curate's best pupil, Pike, "the king of fishermen, or at least the young prince." The boy offers a lesson in fishing which is also a lesson in living. After Gronow boasts of setting wire screens in the brook at each end of his meadow, Penniloe asks the obvious question: Is not that "rather selfish"? Then Pike reveals that the traps are set the wrong way: the fish can swim out but not return. The novel ends with the humbling of Dr. Gronow, but it leaves the reader to reflect on his mistake and the meaning of fishes and streams. To put fish-traps in a brook is to deny the flow and the interrelatedness of life, the constant exchanges by which all creatures live. For life is a stream in *Perlycross*, a movement of all ages and classes through the human seasons, and the stream is fed by nature and grace. Dr. Gronow had screened out both with his traps and his now-dissolving skepticism, depriving himself of fish and of the faith that a fish represents. To live in community is to join the process of giving and receiving, illustrated by the clear stream and the church above it in the novel. A river and a sign of divine giving come together in the title, making one image of mortal experience transformed by the life offered for all to share.

CHAPTER 7

The End of a Career

My difficulty always is to stop, and wisely shut up shop, when I get into full swing of business.[1]

IN the six years between *Perlycross* and his death in 1900, Blackmore published nothing that would save him from being known as a one-book author. While the fame of *Lorna Doone* kept spreading, his last volume of poetry, a collection of short stories, and one more novel won few admirers and cast a dull light over the close of his career. Meredith and Hardy were retiring from novel-writing with far greener laurels; and if Blackmore stood near them in the popular estimation, it was only on the strength of one well-loved story. Yet at his death at least one admirer, the Dartmoor novelist Eden Phillpotts, ranked the three together, apparently to Blackmore's advantage: "In subtlety the others exceeded him; in the quality of a sea-deep, sane humor and tolerance of humanity, he stood far above either."[2] Today, when both Blackmore and Phillpotts are little read outside the West Country, this judgment may sound incomprehensible. Any understanding of it now demands the effort of recognizing shifts in taste and of viewing his work against more durable Victorian novels, like Hardy's, which survived the harsher climate of the twentieth century. But both of these tasks must wait upon the basic one of completing the survey of his forgotten writing.

Neither Blackmore's last volume of poetry nor his book of short stories represented much new creative effort. The verses in *Fringilla* (1895) were nearly all written earlier, though they had been revised since their first publication. Nothing as ambitious as his verse tragedy, *Eric and Karine*, appeared from his earlier volumes; "Fringilla" suggests a finch's chirping, not a swan song. Of his late poetry, the most lively is the humorous autobiographical ballad, "Buscombe: or, the Michaelmas Goose," a happy reminiscence of

116

his West Country boyhood in the vein of "Croker's Hole" and *Perlycross*. The volume came out too soon for any of the verses that he jotted in his notebook after his health began failing. One of these, written in 1897, reads like a modest Victorian variation on John Donne's seduction poem, "The Flea." After rejecting a conventional sexual metaphor of the lover as falcon, the speaker works out a grotesque conceit expressing the shy hesitance of Blackmore's heroes in the presence of the beloved—a far cry from the masculine verbal aggression in Donne:

> Not with stoops of falcon fierce,
> Thy sweet refuge would I pierce—
> Ravenous bird, that strikes his prey,
> Feeds his fill, & sails away.
> Darling, I would rather be
> Yon small spider thou canst see,
> Now in poise of hope & dread,
> Circling down a silver thread,
> Wavering, as he swings upon
> Every breath of pro & con;
> Or with gropings immature
> Coils, recoils, & is not sure
> When to risk his overture.
> So would I thy heart-love win
> Tremulously, & dwell therein.[3]

With the neat contrast of falcon and spider, the lyric is atypical of Blackmore's usually diffuse verse. Headed "Lerodia," this bit of trifling or "foolish talk" is one of the last displays of minor talent in a man who by now realized that mediocrity in poetry is never good enough.[4]

In another genre that demanded concision, Blackmore fared a little better with four rather lengthy short stories in *Tales from the Telling-House* (1896). Unfortunately, the least successful tale would have attracted the most readers because of its title, which the author disliked. "Slain by the Doones" promised a long-awaited sequel to the novel, but it merely treats an incident mentioned by John Ridd in passing—the murder of the retired "Squire" in Bagworthy Forest (ch. 72). Though Ridd by his own account had no part in the episode, he appears in the tale as a purely mythic figure, seen by a young woman as a West Country Hercules, brandishing his club at an opportune moment. Her narrative only serves as a reminder of how lucky Blackmore was in deciding to let John Ridd tell his own story.

More rewards come with the autobiographical writing in the preface to the collection and in the classic fishing story "Croker's Hole." Both recreate scenes from Blackmore's childhood, providing a welcome sense of intimacy with an author who tried to keep his private life private. Yet the self-portrayal is guarded, for the child in the preface appears at the full distance of sixty years from the elderly novelist. Mounted on "a shaggy and stuggy pony," the boy is shown objectively as a separate character from the narrator, in keeping with Blackmore's belief that "the more a writer preserves his own impersonality in his works, the better it is for him & them."[5] But his past self skips over the sixty years as the boy asks his grandfather where the "four sheep are that ought to have R. D. B. on them" and complains of being cheated of "a lot of money." The child sounds decidedly like the father of the man in Blackmore's lawsuits and querulous letters.

The two other stories in this volume are also departures from Blackmore's norm, surprising the reader with unhappy endings. A girl's suicide ends "Frida; or the Lover's Leap," based on a legend of the Wichalse family at Lynton during the English Civil War. "George Bowring, A Tale of Cader Idris," turns upon a Welsh folk-belief in the power of a gold watch to delay the hour of death. The father of a dying peasant girl murders a man to get the watch, but the child dies anyway and the criminal goes unpunished until the last moment of his life. Set in the land of legendary giants and of King Arthur himself, the story conveys a disturbing sense of the uncanny, even down to the events that make the narrator indirectly responsible for the murder. The narrator had planned the trip to Wales and given his friend a gold watch; years earlier he had fallen in love with the woman who married his friend instead. Both stories make Blackmore seem less distant from Hardy than at any time since *Under the Greenwood Tree* and *Cripps, the Carrier*. His darker outlook persists in his next-to-last published story, "Leila; or the Golden Fleece," a romance set in the Caucasus that ends with the shooting of the heroine, who dies in the narrator's arms. Her fate is the one so barely averted in *Lorna Doone*.

The unhappy endings point toward the two subjects that Blackmore considered for his last novel. Originally, he planned a sequel to *Perlycross* based on the troubles of a headstrong peasant girl, Zipporah Tremlett, after she had been adopted by the curate and had run home to the parsonage from a hated boarding school in Exeter. A footnote in the novel held the promise of a sequel, and Blackmore began jotting notes for "Zip, A Tale of Perlycross," in October 1893, scarcely a month after finishing the novel. Eventually, he wrote an opening scene, set in the village in the summer of 1845 and filled with "the scent . . . of peaches from Adjutant Southey's slope, & of honey from the thatched cob-wall, of milk already creaming" in the pail, and "the mellow fragrance of the oatsheaf, rolling home in golden glory, dancing to the harvest song."[6] But after this loving composition of place and a bit of dialogue, the new work stopped. Although Blackmore intended to get on with it throughout 1894, he began tinkering with another subject, one which would take him far from Culmstock to the wilds of the Caucasus.

With a surrender of choice like the one he made while trying to end *Alice Lorraine*, he sent a letter to William Blackwood, leaving the fate of "Zip" to his publisher: "Two stories are in hand with me now, one a vol. of sequel—though concerned with fresh characters of my last novel, 'Perlycross'; the other a more romantic tale of the Surrey Hills, & avoiding Devon altogether. If we could make our arrangements direct, I wd. proceed with either of these, accdg. to your choice."[7] While the author waited at the crossroads between pastoral realism and romance, Blackwood must have considered the mixed reviews of *Perlycross*, the current vogue of romantic adventure novels, and the hope against hope for another *Lorna Doone*. He chose the "romance of the Surrey hills,"[8] and the tale of Zip remained untold. It proved to be the author's last chance to write a novel about the land that held his deepest affection.

After giving up his own power of choice, Blackmore had no right to complain of his publisher's decision, but soon the new task became one of the most frustrating in his long career. Though in November 1895 he spoke of fashioning "a pretty fair plot," he lost confidence by the next month and bewailed "the long sad job," which, he said, "sometimes terrifies me"—all the more because the end of the novel "may never come."[9] He was also feeling pressure to write a fast-moving narrative. After submitting the first number, he halfway apologized to Blackwood for not sounding like Anthony Hope or Rider Haggard: "I cannot bring myself to write in the panting style so popular now; neither can I read anything so written."[10] Then, defending the slow pace of "thoughtful writing" against "the present general taste. . .for hurry & scurry & slash-dash,"[11] he complained of feeling forced "to shun all little bits. . .of description, or weather, or quiet talk or outside nature, because. . .not one reader in ten wd. look at them." These things were essential to his goal of placing "his readers where they may look round, & know where they are, & enjoy the knowledge— without having too much of it."[12] He had realized this goal beautifully in *Perlycross* and might have done so again with the same landscape in "Zip." Now he was stuck with a story of foreign adventure that should have been left to quicker hands. But, as he wrote Blackwood in another context, "enough of wailing. I am a pig under a gate."[13]

Dariel, published in *Blackwood's* in 1896 and 1897, represents an effort to tell adventures thoughtfully, as Joseph Conrad was just learning to do, even while it follows a standard formula for late-Victorian romance. As in Rider Haggard's *She* and other tales of imperial adventure, the novel sends a stalwart young Englishman into an exotic land, not Africa in this case but the Caucasian Mountains. The region had fascinated Blackmore ever since the Crimean War. His friend Hall Caine had visited Russia in 1892, and the recent spate of English translations of Tolstoy might also have reawakened his old interest. Throughout the Victorian era, the Caucasus had a special aura, for ethnologists taught that these mountains were the cradle of European civilization, the mysterious point of racial origin that the hero dreams of in Charles Kingsley's *Alton Locke* (1850). Blackmore resisted the impulse to glamorize both the region and the race, offering instead a balanced view: the land in the novel becomes the setting for immense nobility and for ritualized brutality, where blood feuds are sanctioned and a tribesman may kill an unwanted baby daughter by pouring "red-hot embers" down her throat.[14] Confronting barbarism, no one in *Dariel* objects when the cynical Captain Strogue pronounces his verdict on the Caucasus: "if it was the cradle of the human race, as the ethnologists used to tell us, it was lucky that we tumbled out of it" (360).

Beautiful and terrible, the mountains form a mythic landscape beyond the narrator's familiar Surrey hills. "The Land of Medea" is also "The Land of Prometheus," full of the cruelty, suffering, and nobility that Blackmore finds at the heart of myth and of human nature. More plainly than ever before, he casts a novel in mythic terms to show the conflicting sides of man through the enmity between a twin brother and sister. The Lesghian Prince Imar is the Promethean sufferer; his sister is the Medea and she plots to destroy

him. Both are torn by the passions that make tragedy. Acts of
adultery, revenge, and suicide build the conflict to the point where
the prince faces death at the hand of his unwitting son. Blackmore,
nervous as ever in the neighborhood of tragedy, dreaded that the
story might seem "almost too dark and unnatural," especially since
the "fiend" was a woman.[15] But when the novel opens in Surrey,
the darkness is hidden and the only mythic reality for the young
narrator is romantic love. This hard-working, practical farmer,
George Cranleigh, discovers Dariel, the daughter of the exiled
prince, falls in love, and enters the realm of myth. He will follow
Dariel to the Caucasus when her father returns on a Tolstoyan quest
to educate and to deliver his tribesman from barbarism by teaching
them the Sermon on the Mount. Cranleigh's own task will be to
face the darkness of the mythic realm and, by risking his life, pass
the test of his initiation.

But unlike John Ridd, who makes similar movement from every-
day to mythic experience,[16] this English farmer does not become the
hero of his own story. According to Blackmore, the "real hero" is
the exiled Prince Imar,[17] already initiated through suffering a part
in the blood feuds of the Caucasus, where a "tragedy—and they
have no such thing as a comedy—goes into ten acts at least, and
lasts for generations" (362). At the "heart" of the novel[18] is the story
the prince tells of a chain of revenge that destroyed his marriage; it
recalls the narrative of the Corsican vendetta in Blackmore's first
novel, *Clara Vaughan*. Intended as a warning to the young
Englishman, "Imar's Tale" reveals how love, hatred, and violence
intertwine to create tragedy. Although Imar's sister plotted his ruin,
he makes no claims to innocence. Having killed a suspect and indirectly caused his wife's suicide by doubting her faithfulness, the
exiled prince sums up his past for his untried listener: "I have done
enough of harm, my friend. I have broken up two households; I
have wasted half my tribe in war, and slain a good few Russians.
These you may slay by the thousands, without checking the supply
of them; you are only guilty of their blood, and the tears of those
who loved them. But my own losses taught me what it is to make
others desolate. And the rest of my life, please God, shall go to
redeem the wrongs of wrath and war" (243).

If Imar is heroic, it is not from accomplishing great things but
from accepting responsibility. He does not blame tragedy on fate or
chance or someone's else's villainy. "But who," he asks, "can deny
that there is an inheritance of evil quite beyond our power to ex-

plain?" (246). Facing that inheritance, Imar in middle age has
grown ready to break the chain of revenge by letting the next blow
stop with him. When he waits for it to fall at the climax of the
novel, he acts out the lesson from the Sermon on the Mount that he
wanted to spread among his people. But the sudden, providential
violence of melodrama saves him, and his readiness to suffer evil is
made unnecessary by the conventional heroism of swordplay and
straight shooting.

Blackmore considered "Imar's Tale" as good as anything he had
ever written—"though that may not be anything great"[19]—but the
book as a whole caused him instense dissatisfaction. The ending
seemed "too sudden and jagged"; the story was "full of faults" and
oversized, even after he cut out pages and chapters: if "*Lorna
Doone* is much too long (for a work of real art)," he asked, how
"shall I—in old age—cling to the button-hole of a friend, without
wearing out his good will?"[20] That realization did not ease the pain,
however, when a scornful reviewer in the *Athenaeum* made almost
the same point.[22]

CHAPTER 8

The Question of Blackmore's Achievement

Sometimes I am afraid of doing miserable work, & am reduced to the belief that I have done too much of that character already. . . .[1]

THE novelist's fears of doing "miserable work" invite the question of how well those fears were founded. Certainly they reflect his difficulties in composition and his increasing sense in the 1890s that public taste was going against him. It was, and to try now to evaluate his fiction calls not only for a look at the bases of his self-doubt but also for an awareness of the critical assumptions that elevated realism over romance, and irony over sentiment and humor in the years after his death. A taste for psychological realism prompted the advice in 1897 that he stop trying to represent "modern men and women";[2] a sophisticate's bias against romance in the 1920s led to his dismissal as "that long-winded old concoctor of romantic crudities."[3] By then, "romantic" had become a term of abuse, along with "old" and "long-winded." But as the name of a genre with special conventions and functions, "romance" can be usefully descriptive in dealing with the question of Blackmore's artistry. It names the tradition in which he struggled with the essential elements of his craft: plot and character, setting and style.

In plotting a narrative, Blackmore often seems like something of a crude concoctor. His letters on this point anticipate the objections of his harshest critics. How to conclude a story was a continual problem for him, one which he seldom solved so well that a "sense of the ending" permeates the total work. How could it, when the author began writing with no clear sense of it himself, or changed his mind as he did in *Alice Lorraine*? His uncertainty of direction must have stretched the length of the novels, which in surviving cheap editions of over 400 or 500 close-set pages discourage casual

123

reading. "My difficulty," he confessed, "always is to stop, & wisely
shut up shop, when I get into full swing of business. My plan
enlarges, & my lines fill out & a lot of little cross tracks lead me off,
& I find it harder & harder to pull up."[4] (He has trouble stopping
even here.) With his penchant for digression, for stories within
stories, and clauses within clauses (his "habit of interthought"), he
resembles his garrulous Mrs. Snacks, whose "largeness" of mind
embraced "a family of fifty narratives, during the production of a
single one."[5]

Any plot that emerges from such largeness of mind is apt to be
oddly multilinear, ending arbitrarily without the "verisimilitude"
and "inevitablility" that realism demands.[6] But these terms are
more appropriate to naturalistic fiction than to romantic comedy.
To make them a standard for judging his work is to risk condemning
a whole genre along with the author. Knowing his difficulties in
plotting, Blackmore relied upon the conventions of romance to give
his fiction form, and he seldom tried anything unsanctioned by long
use. The story within a story appears in ancient, Elizabethan, and
nineteenth-century romances, while the tradition of last-minute
rescues and elaborate discovery scenes left the writer free from the
demand to plot out a realistic chain of cause-and-effect events. Trying to write romance during an age of realism, Blackmore had
bravely said, "Improbabilities are nothing";[7] Hardy would say,
more carefully, "It is not improbabilities of incident but improbabilities of character that matter. . . ."[8] In positive terms,
what counts in romance is the author's "rhetorical skill"[9] in filling
the space between beginning and end with appropriate
characterization, lively incidents, and, for Blackmore, loving evoca-
tion of landscape, plant-life, animals, and weather.

His most famous book proves the wisdom of accepting romantic
conventions in order to enjoy the humor, excitement, and quickened sense of life that floods John Ridd's narrative. But *Lorna
Doone* is the most openly romantic of Blackmore's novels and one
of the earliest. The rise of realism in the eras of Thackeray, George
Eliot, and Henry James made any suspension of disbelief increasingly lowbrow, if not more difficult. Addressing readers with a
"discriminating" rather than an "omnivorous taste in fiction," a
hostile critic in 1887 could not forgive Blackmore's use of "matters
only suited to a fairy tale."[10] The crime would look especially glar-
ing in books like *Springhaven* which are not obvious romances; in
fact, Blackmore's characterization and his attention to local and

historical detail sometimes suggest attempts at realism. The contrast between a realistic texture and an improbable romantic plot bewildered even a friendly reviewer of *Cripps, the Carrier,* leaving him caught between his delight in the book and his sense of its absurdity. To summarize a novel with an abduction in Oxfordshire, three rescues from imminent death, and an elaborate discovery scene would "turn the story . . . into ridicule."[11] His resource was to separate the plot from the "charm" of characterization, dialogue, and description.

Such indulgence still is easy enough for an unpretentious book like *Cripps* but very difficult when the characters lack interest and the plot seems only a means of prolonging tedium. At his worst, Blackmore deserves the parody of *Kit and Kitty* in which the elderly orchardman says, "Bear up, Chris my boy. We're all right because we're in a novel."[12] They have every reason to feel snug, for Blackmore's authorial providence is at least as predictably protective as Hardy's fate is destructive. But unless the book offers something more than the plot, the price of their security will be the reader's boredom, unrelieved by stilted pages of genteel conversation or the narrator's grouching about Free Trade.

In itself, the romantic plot of loss and recovery neither breaks nor makes Blackmore's fiction. He can handle it impressively in *Lorna Doone* and *Perlycross,* perfunctorily in *Alice Lorraine,* and comically in *Cripps,* but the success of his books depends upon more than this ancient pattern. Much depends upon his characters, and here he offends the canons of realism in a way that Hardy does not. The offense comes mainly with his heroes and heroines, who fall in love at first or second sight, seldom stray from their romantic goals, and behave with the decorum of courtly lovers. From the modern viewpoint, they are stereotypes, unbelievably simple when set beside the "real" characters of Henry James and George Eliot. With its tacit assumption that to be "real" is to be complex and probably confused, the modern view was attacked by late-Victorian defenders of romance, who complained that James's endlessly introspective women and "emasculated" men were only the "specimens of an overwrought age":[13] they were not embodiments of essential humanity. The real man or woman was altogether different—simple, straightforward, even heroic; and "any seeming idealization of character," according to one admirer of Blackmore's heroines, was "only the subtle grasping of the true identity."[14]

The realist's view triumphed in this controversy, and it still puts readers of Blackmore, Haggard, or Stevenson on the defensive. But the issue is not whether John Ridd is more or less real than some Prufrockian center of consciousness in Henry James. The basic questions in romance are whether and why the hero and heroine appeal to the reader. The answers will reflect individual tastes, obviously, but much depends on how well these characters are tested. Whether they are comic like Daphnis and Chloe or tragic like Romeo and Juliet, the hero and heroine must be tested in order to act out the experience of romantic love. Blackmore's mistake after *Lorna Doone* was to shield his well-behaved young ladies and gentlemen until they rarely seem vulnerable to the dangers or the silliness of the experience. The threats to their happiness seem manufactured for the occasion in *Christowell* and *Kit and Kitty,* while the return to perilous romance in *Dariel* partly fails because the lovers do not face dangers together in scenes like those in the Doone Valley. By playing an overprotective providence, Blackmore almost deprives the young couples of their essential role, for love without risk is hardly romantic. Certainly it makes an inadequate plot for a long novel.

But most of Blackmore's later fiction takes shape from a more public and less stylized action than a love story. The love between a young hero and heroine becomes only one thread in a design that represents the experience of a whole community. If *Christowell,* *Springhaven,* and *Perlycross* seem unusually digressive and baggy, that is because the community is the protagonist. A multitude of characters and incidents is essential to the story. To represent country life in a single, steadily focused plot, as Hardy does, calls for an immense effort of stylization, not only in paring away lesser characters and details but also in speeding up rural time to cover the career of one central figure. Since rural experience is marked by the movement from seedtime to seedtime, a story of the countryside naturally moves with the seasons, like *Under the Greenwood Tree,* the loosest-knit of Hardy's novels. Blackmore times his plots by the seasons, letting the movement from winter to summer support his stories of loss and renewal. Even then, the full-scale novels of community nearly break under the weight of accumulated characters. But at the very point of threatened artistic chaos lies the earthy treasure of his fiction—the farmers, fishermen, sailors, servants, landladies, shopkeepers, and schoolchildren who more than make up for the tedium in the squire's garden or the vicar's parlor. For every fainting heroine there is an unblushing Betty Muxworthy or a

Mrs. Tugwell; for every modest hero there is a John Fry, a Clerk Channing, or a grumbling Uncle Cornelius. These little people, if not always the salt of the earth, are the needed seasoning for Blackmore's idealizing imagination. [15]

Each of these characters brings to his fiction a personal landscape, a field of being, charged with particular human energies. Not only does the heroine have her springtime bower and the villain his waste moorland: the little people also fill spaces that both illuminate and reflect their presence. In *Perlycross* alone, the interplay between person, place, and season occurs at the rotting mill in December where Mrs. Tremlett is dying, and along the ditch of dead weeds haunted by the half-witted poacher; it can be felt on the morning of melting frost in the potato field where the blacksmith tells his scary story and on the May morning of the closing fishing scene. Being, for his characters, is the concrete act of filling a certain spot in time and space, weighting both with individual human presences. Finding "the very sap and scent of country life" in Blackmore's stories, Eden Phillpotts singled out his gift for "noting the details of rural scenery through the procession of the seasons, and setting them forth, as only an artist can, in their due relation to the mass of mountains, to the volume of rivers, to the life of men and women." [16] The last phrase points to the achievement that makes Blackmore a novelist, and not a describer only, of the countryside.

But the elaborate wordpainting which Hardy and Hopkins also admired can prove an obstacle to any reader who wants to get on with the story. Blackmore himself realized the danger and disciplined an early impulse to outdo Ruskin. Even so, his verbal landscapes sometimes sound showy and precious, like George Meredith's, and suggest a lack of Hardy's genius for keeping description subordinate to the narrative as a whole. Their contrast with Hardy's landscapes makes obvious an essential feature of Blackmore's vision. His is openly impressionistic, fluid, and responsive to change, while Hardy's is poetic in a quieter, more stable way and focused on longer-lasting marks of being. The famous description of Blackmore Vale in *Tess of the d'Urbervilles* (ch. 2) presents a landscape "like a map" before an unspecified traveler, outlines its enduring pattern, and treats its colors as if they would always stay the same. The pattern consists of a "network of dark green threads" formed by the hedgerows, with "a broad rich mass of grass and trees, mantling minor hills and dales within the major." The atmosphere is unchanging; the scene stays essentially static as it is laid out in a series of main clauses that assert being only. Things either are or seem; they do not appear in distinctive action.

A more impressionistic writer could never conclude, with Hardy's finality, that "such is the Vale of Blackmore." For any landscape, even this green Dorset one, changes with the light, the seasons, and the weather. Blackmore treats change as essential. To evoke the movement of things, his verbs are active and his long sentences eddy and flow with the large variety of the movement. Describing a huge view from east Dartmoor in *Christowell,* he puts a more specific traveler on the scene, gives him a good breakfast (since a person's mood colors what he sees), and lets him look outdoors by the "light of an average morning." At once, the scene begins to act. Beyond the stable landmarks of Exeter Cathedral, Powderham Castle, and the coastline, "the broad sweep of the English Channel glistens, or darkens, with the moods above it, from the Dorset headlands to the Start itself. Before he has time to make sure of all this, the grand view wavers, and the colours blend; some parts retire and some come nearer, and lights and shadows flow and flit, like the wave and dip of barley, feathering to a gentle July breeze" (19). Then, just as Blackmore seems most emulous of Ruskin and Turner, he stops without even saying which colors are blending. He has evoked the movement of a landscape, not a static pattern.

Furthering the sense of movement is his rhythmic phrasing and echoing of like sounds. His cadences are far more emphatic than Hardy's, not only in the metrical passages of *Cradock Nowell* and *Lorna Doone,* but here in "the flow and flit" of barley or the "sweep of upland" in *Perlycross,* "black in some places with bights of fired furze, but streaked with long alleys of green, where the flames had not fed, or the rains had wept them off" (128). Hardy does not write with this springiness of rhythm; Meredith comes closer to it in his moments of ecstatic prose. But Blackmore achieved his distinctive lilt at the risk of sounding self-conscious, like Meredith, as in this passage from *Christowell,* when the eye moves down the slopes of Fingle Vale: "Deep in the wooded bottom quiver, like a clue of gossamer, sunny threads of the twisted river, wafted through the lifts of gloom" (152). Rhyming at one point, the first three cadences keep the rhythm restless with their weak final syllables, until the eye returns from the swift water to the still "lifts of gloom."

The trouble with this bit of buried Tennyson is the way it calls attention to itself. Momentarily the style counts for more than either the setting or the story. Poetic description continues in the next paragraph until the narrator, as if embarrassed by his own eloquence, undercuts it all with humor. Scenic grandeur now contrasts with low-bred tourists' cries of "come here, Harry," and "oh larks, Matilda" in the degenerate present—unlike the time of the story when "Our good British race had not yet been driven, to pant up hill, and perspire down dale, for the sake of saying that they had done it." Humor dissipates the poetry and eventually leads back to the characters, who are still miles from Fingle Vale. Rather than advancing the plot, as description generally does in Hardy, this little essay into and against the picturesque serves as a resting place between narrative and dialogue. But to stop and look round a landscape is a delight in Blackmore, who tries hard to make it worthwhile and more than matches his lapses into metrical pomposity with cadences elsewhere of strong poetic force. When John Ridd tells how the reapers swept the field "like half a wedge of wildfowl" or describes the great snowdrift "rolling and curling beneath the violent blast," the language moves with the energy of nature itself, and the effect seems worth the rhetorical effort. Hardy can also evoke this power, but not with Blackmore's springing rhythms and the lilt of a narrator's voice.

In depicting the intricate life of nature, Blackmore can stand comparison with any British novelist of his century. But only here, and perhaps in humor, does he surpass his master in historical fiction, Sir Walter Scott, with whom he was compared more often than with Hardy. Like Scott, he helped to clothe a land in its own history and legend. But he writes from a narrower perspective and covers far less time and space. Scott's vision is not only wider but more balanced. Scott does not grumble about contemporary politics like the omniscient narrator of *Springhaven;* he sounds far more Olympian, at once more detached from political issues and more understanding of them than Blackmore, and he speaks with far less eccentricity of rhythm, imagery, and syntax. His fame rests on many historical novels, while Blackmore won popular success with only one book. As an avowed "romance" and not "an historical novel," *Lorna Doone* stays closer to local legend than to the national events that would have concerned Scott. Though Judge Jeffreys and James II make brief appearances, Monmouth's Rebellion happens almost entirely offstage, becoming real only when a peace-loving young farmer strays among the dead and wounded after the Battle of Sedgemoor. The author of *Waverley* would have put him nearer to the intrigue and the fighting.

When Blackmore does invite comparison with Scott in *Springhaven,* his greatest achievement is not in portraying Nelson or Napoleon but in making the village a microcosm of the nation. As a historical novelist, he is less concerned with grand events than with their repercussions among the little people in a particular neighborhood. Writing of fishermen on the Sussex or Yorkshire coast or of farmfolk on Exmoor, he brings to life the manners, customs, and speech of people whom the noted historians long ignored. Scott provided a model for extending the historical vision to include ordinary folk, and Blackmore learned the lesson so well that Victorian reviewers saw his books as a means of holding images of rural life against the time when all the villages in England should have died out or spread into towns. [17] Although these pictures need balanced by less humorous and romantic ones, they form his most impressive approach to history.

At the other end of the century from Scott, the popular romancers who came after Blackmore show less concern with rural characters and seldom linger as long among pastoral landscapes. From *Lorna Doone,* Robert Louis Stevenson might have learned to create a distinctive voice for the narrator of *Kidnapped,* but he could have been taught as much by several other classics of Victorian fiction. What distinguishes John Ridd from Pip or David Copperfield, Henry Esmond or Harry Richmond, is his rustic voice, which at moments in the early chapters sounds less like these gentlemanly ones than it does like Huck Finn's. Huck and John both express the delights of the open air, of fishing, swimming, and eating; and when John as a boy passes a man's corpse hanging upon Exmoor, he responds with Huck's sympathy to the dead sheep-stealer: "I was sorry for Red Jem, and wanted to know more about him, and whether he might not have avoided this miserable end, and what his wife and children thought about it, if indeed he had any." But as a stylist, Huck lacks the earlier narrator's admiration for Shakespeare and his exposure to Latin syntax. A closer echoing of Ridd's voice comes in John Meade Falkner's *Moonfleet* (1898), narrated by an eighteenth-century Dorset man named John Trenchard, who tells his adventures in long, loosely constructed sentences that suggest something of the style and tone of *Lorna Doone.*

Blackmore may have influenced the romantic regional fiction of the United States, where his story of outlaws was immensely popular. Reduced to its simplest form, as in a movie or a classic comic, his masterpiece suggests a number of American Westerns, though when read unabridged—with the seasoned farmer telling his youthful adventures—the book is so unique that not even its author could do another like it. A classic Western, Owen Wister's *Virginian* (1902), lacks the rustic narrator, but it has a strong cowboy hero, a lovely heroine, lots of carefully recorded dialect, a scene of frontier merrymaking, and its own equivalent of the Doones in some marauding Indians and a nasty villain, whom the hero deals with on the evening before the wedding, instead of just afterward as in *Lorna Doone*. Still more reminiscent of the stage properties and the conflict upon Exmoor is Harold Bell Wright's *Shepherd of the Hills* (1907), set in the Ozarks near Branson, Missouri. The novel has a band of outlaws and a gigantic hero to match John Ridd in feats of strength and skill at wrestling. The style is fulsomely picturesque in rendering both the mountain landscape and the native dialect. A best-seller, like *Lorna Doone* the book still promotes tourism, bringing thousands each year to the summer pageant, the motels, and the gift shops of "The Shepherd of the Hills Country."

As a writer of less romantic narratives than *Lorna Doone*, Blackmore is more closely linked with the early George Eliot, whose *Adam Bede* (1859) helped to start the regional novel in England, and with Hardy, who entered the field with *Under the Greenwood Tree* in 1872, after Blackmore had already dealt with rural life in North Devon, Hampshire, and Somerset. Independently of each other, they started exploring the countryside of southern England. At the time each began admiring the other's work in 1875, the two men were not so far apart as they would seem by the 1890s, when they stopped writing novels. *Under the Greenwood Tree* could have been the model for *Cripps, the Carrier* and the dance in *Christowell;* Hardy found it "almost absurd" that he had not read *Lorna Doone* before writing *Far from the Madding Crowd*, for both stories represent shepherding and farming, the festivity of harvest, and the subtler changes of plant-life and weather. Drawn to the past, to folklore and West Country speech, both writers were conscious rural historians, trying, in Hardy's words, "to preserve . . . a fairly true record of a vanishing life."[18]

Both saw it vanishing, but where Hardy's vision turned bitter and tragic, Blackmore's remained comic, despite his anger at the fate of British agriculture once the nation began to rely upon imported food. Hardy went on to show the decline of the village culture; Blackmore almost never dealt with it directly and seldom set his novels later than 1840. Only the grumbling asides of his narrators suggest the contrast between present rural distress and the stability of an imagined past. In the grief, irritation, and lameness of old age, he kept celebrating an out-dated vision of rural society along with the growth of things in fiction, while tending the apple and pear trees of his unprofitable orchard. Often disappointed, he never reached Hardy's conviction "that it was better not to have lived than face the ordeal of life as a conscious being."[19] He did not blame suffering upon an Aeschylean "President of the Immortals" (Gladstone was a more likely scapegoat), or write as coolly as Hardy about the coming of a new springtime: "Another year's instalment of flowers, leaves, nightingales, thrushes, finches, and such ephemeral creatures, took up their positions where only a year ago others had stood in their place when these were nothing more than germs and inorganic particles."[20] To the last, he stayed true to his love for "green and growing things," the "secret of his in-spiration."[21]

Knowing and amiring both writers as old men, their successor in West Country fiction, Eden Phillpotts, dedicated his first Dartmoor novel to Blackmore and eulogized him in 1904 at the dedication of the memorial in Exeter Cathedral. In the fifty-six years that remained of his life, Phillpotts saw Hardy emerge as the classic novelist of the English countryside, while virtually all of Blackmore but *Lorna Doone* slipped from the public eye. Having once ranked his master with Hardy and Meredith, Phillpotts in 1951 was still praising "Blackmore's vision, wisdom, and humour."[22] This praise should count, coming from an author whose twenty Dartmoor novels form an impressive portrait of a region, and whose vision differs significantly from Blackmore's own. Agnostic and rationalistic, Phillpotts based his guarded optimism on evolution, not on faith in divine providence. His novels sometimes end as starkly as Hardy's, and they depart from the niceties of Victorian romance. Yet he could admire both older writers and find, as a realist, what he wanted from English fiction in Blackmore—"a true picture of our national life and character."[23] The old-fashioned framework of romantic comedy never stopped him from looking at the picture, nor should it stop anyone else. As Hardy said, "Some natures become vocal at tragedy, some are made vocal by comedy, and it seems to me that to whichever of these aspects of life a writer's instinct for expression more readily responds, to that he should allow it to respond."[24] Blackmore deserves the allowance that Hardy wanted for himself.

What matters, after all, is not the gilded Victorian frame but the life within the picture. If time has erased or painted over the world that Blackmore remembered, the changes make his vision all the more worth preserving. The lost, cart-horse's pace of village life can still be felt in *Cripps, the Carrier* and *Perlycross*, though the wheel-ruts have long been paved and milk-lorries roar between the hedgerows. Where John Ridd turned to wade up Bagworthy Water, touring coaches unload beside a gift shop; and in the gorge at Fingle Bridge a shop and inn provide shelter for any picnickers caught in rains like those that spoiled Julia Touchwood's "gipseying" in *Christowell*. Tourism long ago replaced fishing as the major industry at Flamborough Head, the Yorkshire setting of *Mary Anerley*, and the current heroes of the North Sea are more likely to be the men on the oil rigs than any dashing smugglers. But Blackmore's vision is not entirely of things past. The sea breaks against the cliffs, snow drifts on the moors, and men still fish. The green patchwork of the Devon hills still nourishes sheep and cows; where farmyards hum with milking-machines and high-banked lanes resound with tractors, the ancient pastoral work of man goes on, despite the Common Market imports of butter, lamb, and bacon which would have dismayed the Victorian enemy of Free Trade. Fewer now, the thatched houses still stand in sheltered combes and in the villages that are always said to be dying. The thatch sprouts television aerials as well as moss, and the calm BBC voice in the low-beamed sitting-rooms tells of more abductions and murders than the Doones ever inflicted upon Exmoor. While life goes on this way, with times of peace and of terror in the long "procession of the seasons," Blackmore has a part with greater artists, like Hardy and Wordsworth, who teach "our eyes to see."[25]

Notes and References

Preface

1. Conrad to William Blackwood, 4 September 1897, commenting on Blackmore's last novel, *Dariel*, in *Letters to William Blackwood and David S. Meldrum*, ed. William Blackburn (Durham, 1958), p. 8.
2. *The History of the English Novel*, IX (1936; rpt. New York, 1966), p. 293.
3. *A History of English Literature, 1830 - 1880*, II (1920; rpt. London, 1965), p. 319.

Chapter One

1. To Edward Marston in 1895, quoted in Waldo Hilary Dunn, *R. D. Blackmore, The Author of "Lorna Doone"* (London, 1956), p. 23.
2. Arthur Joseph Munby in Derek Hudson, *Munby: Man of Two Worlds* (London, 1972), p. 396.
3. See Dunn, p. 273, and Blackmore's letter to John Blackwood, 16 January 1872, National Library of Scotland (henceforth NLS), and to Alexander Macmillan, 27 January 1866, in William E. Buckler, "Blackmore's Novels before 'Lorna Doone,' " *Nineteenth-Century Fiction*, X (December 1955): 184.
4. Sec review of "A Sermon Preached at the Parish Church of Tormohun, on Friday Nov. 5, 1841," *Gentleman's Magazine*, CXVI (1842): 521 - 22.
5. See Sally Jones, "A Lost Leader: R.D. Blackmore and 'The Maid of Sker,' " *Anglo-Welsh Review*, XXV (Autumn 1975): 34.
6. A. B. Blackmore in "R. D. Blackmore and Culmstock," *Devon Life*, VI (May 1970): 14, published the fact of this child's existence, dispelling the belief, held by Dunn, that there had been an infant daughter of John Blackmore who died during his first marriage. See also the Blackmore family tree, compiled by Douglas W. Blackmore and R. B. Blackmore, dated April 1966, in the Westcountry Studies Library, Exeter (henceforth the library will be identified as WSL).
7. Devon Record Office, Exeter.
8. To unnamed correspondent, 1 July 1875, in Dunn, p. 27.
9. To Mary Ann Blackmore, John Blackmore's devoted sister, from Bushey, Herts., 25 September 1827, in Devon Record Office.

10. See Dunn, p. 42.

11. Ibid.

12. See John Blackmore's letter to the Dean and Chapter of Exeter Cathedral, 9 June 1836, Exeter Cathedral Library. He states that the choir had proved "very troublesome" to his predecessor.

13. John Blackmore to Ralph Barnes, Clerk for the Dean and Chapter, 7 March 1839, Exeter Cathedral Library.

14. Letter to Alexander Macmillan, 25 March 1864, British Museum.

15. To Mary Frances Gordon, January 13, in Dunn, p. 44.

16. Quoted in Dunn, p. 29.

17. *Perlycross: A Tale of the Western Hills* (London, 1894), p. 9.

18. *Mary Anerley: A Yorkshire Tale* (1880; rpt. London, 1894), p. 83.

19. See Dunn, p. 42.

20. M. L. Banks, *Blundell's Worthies* (London, 1904), p. 155. (The only nickname I have seen for him is "Doddy" on a school notebook.)

21. See Dunn, p. 56.

22. Robert Lawson to Blackmore, 13 March 1890, Hench Collection, University of Virginia (henceforth the library is identified as UV).

23. To Edwin Jacobs, 14 November 1894, quoted by the kind permission of Rev. Michael Hancock, Vicar of Culmstock. The parish owns Blackmore's two letters to Jacobs.

24. See S. M. Ellis, *Wilkie Collins, Le Fanu, and Others* (London, 1931), p. 119, quoting F. J. Snell, *Blundell's: A Short History of a Famous West Country School* (London, 1928), p. 143.

25. To John Blackwood, 17 January 1872, NLS.

26. "Fragmenta," in Notebook at the University of Exeter Library.

27. *Alice Lorraine: A Tale of the South Downs* (1875; rpt. London, n.d.), p. 373.

28. See his letter to Alfred Pinto-Leite, 13 January 1866, UV.

29. *Alice Lorraine*, p. 186.

30. To Alexander Macmillan, 2 March 1866, in Buckler, p. 186.

31. To Mrs. Paul Hamilton Hayne, 4 May 1888, in Dunn, p. 262.

32. From lists of examination questions in Blackmore's Oxford papers, UV.

33. In Dunn, p. 30.

34. To Showell Rogers, 29 November 1897, UV.

35. To Munby, 18 January 1885, in Dunn, p. 164.

36. See Dunn, p. 76.

37. No. 1430 (24 March 1855), p. 347.

38. 3 February 1855. The diary is in the British Museum.

39. An enigmatic entry for May 17 suggests that Blackmore's father stopped by to see the couple, though the meeting could have occurred at the Inner Temple: "Govr. comes back from Kent,—gives £2.—Good bye.—Fine night. . . ."

40. See Hudson, *Munby. . .*, p. 169, and Dunn, p. 77.

41. Dunn, p. 85. For details about this will, which was proven 4

November 1857, and Blackmore's own will, I am indebted to Vera Ledger, F.S.A. When Blackmore's father died in 1858, most of his money was held in trust for Henry, the novelist's elder brother. Richard was named an executor by his father.

42. See Kenneth Budd, *The Last Victorian: R. D. Blackmore and His Novels* (London, 1960), p. 29, and Dunn, p. 97.

43. Hudson, pp. 169, 396.

44. See Ellis, p. 126.

45. Hall Caine, *My Story* (London, 1908), p. 298.

46. Hudson, p. 212.

47. To Alfred Pinto-Leite, 1868, UV.

48. To William Taylor, 2 March [1894].

49. "Apology, 1871," in Blackmore's *Georgics of Virgil* (London, 1886), p. 67; first published 1871.

50. To Edward Marston, no date, in Dunn, p. 99. See also Sir Herbert Warren, intro. to *Lorna Doone* (London, 1922), p. viii; first published 1913.

51. To Mrs. Kathe Freilegrath Kroeker, 4 July 1877, UV.

52. Dunn, pp. 92, 98.

53. From unsigned manuscript notes dated "Sat. April 17, 1897," UV.

54. To Mr. Masters, 27 July 1897, UV.

55. See H. M. Alder to Blackmore, 25 April 1885, UV.

56. Robert Marston to Blackmore, June 1892, UV.

57. To Showell Rogers, 30 December 1895, and to Mackenzie Bell, 24 May 1899, UV.

58. *Saturday Review*, XXXIX (15 May 1875): 634.

59. To Mackenzie Bell, 1 April 1897, UV.

60. *Athenaeum*, No. 3,658 (4 December 1897): 782.

61. See Dunn, p. 233. A settlement out of court saved Blackmore from the ruin that he feared.

62. To Alfred Pinto-Leite, 23 December 1865, in Dunn, pp. 219, 220.

63. To Edward Marston, February 1888, in Dunn, p. 251.

64. To F. B. Doveton, 8 February 1888, UV.

65. To Lucy Derby, 20 February 1888, in Dunn, p. 252.

66. To Alfred Pinto-Leite, 30 May 1888, UV.

67. The will is dated 28 July 1897 and was proven 7 March 1900.

68. Henry Snowden Ward to Eva Pinto-Leite, 7 April 1908, UV. Ward approved her resolve to keep Blackmore's "private life, *memoirs*, diary, & letters as a closed book," but he said, "No matter that can be properly used to illuminate the text & add to its interest, should be suppressed."

69. Budd, p. 125.

Chapter Two

1. Blackmore explains "Melanter" in a letter of 1882 to an unidentified correspondent, Dunn, p. 80.

2. For a chapter on the Spasmodic School, see Jerome Hamilton

Buckley, *The Victorian Temper* (1952; rpt. London, 1966).

3. *My Story*, p. 302.

4. Anders Fryxell, *The History of Sweden*, trans. Anne von Schoultz, II (London, 1844), p. 269.

5. Walter Johnson, in the introduction to his translation of *Eric XIV* in Strindberg's *Vasa Trilogy* (Seattle, 1959), p. 246.

6. *Poems by Melanter* (London, 1854), p. 48; subsequent page references appear in the text.

7. *Athenaeum*, No. 1430 (24 March 1855): 347.

8. From the revised version in *Fringilla* (London, 1895), p. 15.

9. On the sacrifice of a maiden to the Nile, see Sir James Frazer, *Adonis, Attis, and Osiris* (London, 1907), p. 290.

10. See George Steiner, "In Bluebeard's Castle—Some Notes toward a Re-definition of Culture," *Listener*, LXXXV (18 March 1971): 329.

11. Henry Kingsley, *Ravenshoe* (1862; rpt. London, 1909), p. 325.

12. *Spectator*, XXVIII (20 January 1855): 78.

13. See Paul Fussell (drawing upon Barbara Tuchman), *The Great War and Modern Memory* (New York, 1975), pp. 21 - 22, 175.

14. *The Bugle of the Black Sea* (London, 1855), p. 101; subsequent page references are in the text.

15. "Lyril Mohun," *Epullia* (London, 1854), p. 22.

16. "A Song at Balaclava," *Bugle*, p. 65.

17. "Sicilian Hours," *Dublin University Magazine*, XLVI (August 1855): 201.

18. Ibid.

19. On the influence of Theocritus and Virgil, see Quincy Guy Burris, *Richard Doddridge Blackmore: His Life and Novels, University of Illinois Studies in Language and Literature*, XV (Urbana, 1930), pp. 69ff.

20. The two poems are "Mount Arafa" in *Poems by Melanter* and "Kadisha" in *Dublin University Magazine*, XLVII (May and June, 1856): 549 - 54, 696 - 701. Both were reprinted in *Fringilla*.

21. *The Georgics of Virgil*, p. 63. Books I and II were first published as *The Farm and Fruit of Old* in 1862.

22. See *Perlycross*, p. 270, where he calls Devon speech "Ionic."

23. *Westminster Review*, LXXXVII (January 1867): 260.

24. "The Georgics of Virgil," *Spectator*, XLIV (23 September 1871): 1155. As late as 1932 an edition of this work received praise in the *Times Literary Supplement*, No. 1,580 (12 May): 346.

25. See Budd, p. 30.

26. To Showell Rogers, 21 September 1895, UV.

27. *Cradock Nowell: A Tale of the New Forest* (1866; revised 1873; rpt. London, 1877), p. 193; subsequent page references appear in the text.

28. To John Blackwood, 6 February 1873, NLS. For Bulwer-Lytton's defences of romantic fiction, see Edwin M. Eigner, *The Metaphysical Novel in England and America: Dickens, Bulwer, Melville and Hawthorne* (Berkeley, 1978).

29. Moses Hadas, in the introduction to his translation of *An Ethiopian Romance* (Ann Arbor: 1957), p. viii.

30. See Buckler, p. 174: *Cassell's Illustrated Family Paper* ran *The Purpose of a Life* from 12 March 1864 to 6 August 1864.

31. Aeschylus, *The Libation Bearers*, trans. Richard Lattimore (New York, 1967), p. 115. Sir Herbert Warren notes the classical epigraphs in Blackmore in his introduction to the Oxford edition of *Lorna Doone* (1913; rpt. London, 1922), p. xviii.

32. *Clara Vaughan* (1864; rpt. London, 1881), p. 69; subsequent page references appear in the text.

33. *Examiner*, No. 2,936 (7 May 1864): 293; see Buckler, p. 177.

34. *Spectator*, XXXVII (26 March 1864):363.

35. *Athenaeum*, No. 1905 (30 April 1864): 610.

36. To Alexander Macmillan, 6 November 1863, Buckler, p. 170.

37. A mangawazzle is a mangold wurzel, a variety of beet.

38. *Spectator*, p. 364.

39. To Macmillan, 28 March 1864, Buckler, p. 176; and to John Blackwood, 27 January 1871, NLS.

40. To Macmillan, 28 March 1864, Buckler, p. 177.

41. See Budd, p. 40.

42. *The New Forest: Its History and Scenery* (1863; rpt. London, 1867), p. 5.

43. The parson is named for the Rev. Joseph Rosdew, the vicar of Bushey when Blackmore's father served there as curate and received from him the gold watch which Blackmore mentions in his will. The novelist's uncle, the Rev. Henry Hey Knight, is supposed to be the model for this character. Dunn, p. 40, cites the source for the name "Cradock Nowell" on a monument in the church at Newton Nottage.

44. Kingsley, *Ravenshoe*, p. 163.

45. *Westminster Review*, LXXXVII (January 1867): 260.

46. Ibid.

47. From Macmillan, 25 January 1866, *Letters to Macmillan*, ed. Simon Nowell-Smith (London, 1967), p. 66.

48. To Macmillan, 27 January 1866, Buckler, p. 184.

49. O. A. J. Cockshut, *The Unbelievers: English Agnostic Thought, 1840 - 1890* (London, 1964), p. 161.

50. To Macmillan, 2 March 1866, Buckler, p. 186.

51. To Macmillan, 27 January 1866, Buckler, p. 184.

52. To Macmillan, 19 December 1864, Buckler, p. 180.

53. See Buckler, p. 185.

54. H. Snowden Ward gives a synopsis of this story, which bears little resemblance to Blackmore's plot, in his introduction to the Doone-land edition of *Lorna Doone* (London, 1908). Ward's source claimed that Blackmore admitted his indebtedness to the story, but in a letter to W. C. Forman the novelist denied having seen it (16 September 1891, UV). More recent source-hunting has been stimulated by reports of a ghost of a woman

supposedly shot at the altar on her wedding day, like Lorna Doone. The ghost of Mary Whiddon was reported 10 July 1971 at Whiddon Park, Chagford, on Dartmoor. Her seventeenth-century memorial in the Chagford Church contains these lines:

> Reader woulds't know who here is laid
> Behold a Matron yet a Maid
> A modest looke a pious heart
> A Mary for the better part—
> But drie thine eies Why wilt thou weepe
> Such damsells do not die but sleepe.

Particulars are on file at the Westcountry Studies Library, Exeter.

Chapter Three

1. *Lorna Doone: An Exmoor Romance*, Chapter 42. In view of the many editions, subsequent quotations will be identified by chapter in the text, except when they are from the first edition of 1869. Blackmore completed his main revisions in time for the illustrated edition of 1883; I am quoting from the Doone-land edition with introduction by H. Snowden Ward (London, 1908).

2. See Oakeley's informative and polemical brochure, *The Facts on which R. D. Blackmore Based Lorna Doone* (Williton, Somerset, n.d.), and Nicolai Tolstoy's "Location of 'Glen Doone,'" *Blackmore Studies*, No. 1 (1969): 6. Longer illustrated guides to the region include L. B. Thornicroft's *Story of the Doones in Fact, Fiction, and Photo*, revised and enlarged (Taunton, 1944); and S. H. Burton's *Lorna Doone Trail* (Williton, Somerset, 1975).

3. Hudson, p. 295.

4. *Anatomy of Criticism* (1957; rpt. New York, 1967), p. 138.

5. *Cradock Nowell*, final paragraph as reworded for the 1873 edition.

6. See Mircea Eliade, *Rites and Symbols of Initiation*, trans. Willard Trask (1958; rpt. New York, 1965), p. 110; and Karl Kerényi, *Eleusis: Archetypal Image of Mother and Daughter* trans. Ralph Manheim (London, 1967), p. 33. In an essay that Blackmore might have read, Charles M. Kent assumed that the abduction of Persephone was reenacted in his "Glimpse into the Eleusinian Mysteries," *Blackwood's Magazine*, LXXIII (1853): 185 - 206.

7. Quoted by Kerényi, p. 15, from Cicero's treatise *On the Laws*, II, xiv.

8. Joseph Campbell, *The Hero with a Thousand Faces* (1947; rpt. New York, 1967), p.11

9. *Athenaeum*, No. 2164 (17 April 1869): 534.

10. To Blackmore, 8 June 1875, *The Collected Letters of Thomas Hardy,* ed. Richard L. Purdy and Michael Millgate, I (Oxford, 1978), p. 37.

11. "An Illustrated Edition of 'Lorna Doone,'" *Art Journal,* XXXIV (1883): 375.

12. *The Letters of Gerard Manley Hopkins to Robert Bridges,* ed. Claude Colleer Abbott (London, 1935), p. 238; and *Further Letters of Gerard Manley Hopkins, Including his Correspondence with Coventry Patmore,* ed. Claude Colleer Abbott (London, 1938), p. 241.

13. See Kenneth Budd, "*Lorna Doone:* a 'Christian Novel,'" *Blackmore Studies,* No. 1 (1969): 2.

14. Review in *Athenaeum,* op. cit.

15. See Maxwell H. Goldberg's introduction to *Lorna Doone* (New York, 1956), p. vii.

16. Kilvert's Diary, ed. William Plomer, II (London, 1961), p. 283.

17. "E. T." [Jessie Chambers], *Lawrence: A Personal Reminiscence* (London, 1935), p. 96.

18. To Blackmore, 20 January 1876, UV; for further signs of the book's appeal to such diverse figures as e.e. cummings, Laurens van der Post, and Al Capp, see R. L. Blackmore's fine introduction to the Everyman edition of *Lorna Doone* (London, 1966).

19. "Croker's Hole," *Tales from the Telling House* (London, 1896), p. 226; the story first appeared in 1879.

20. See Dunn, p. 56.

21. Introduction to *Lorna Doone* (1913; rpt. London, 1922), p. xi.

22. For evidence of the Victorian fascination with power, see Walter E. Houghton, *The Victorian Frame of Mind, 1830 - 1870* (New Haven, 1957), pp. 196ff.

23. *Westward Ho!* (1855; rpt. London, n.d.), p. 64; and Henry R. Harrington, "Charles Kingsley's Fallen Athlete," *Victorian Studies,* XXI (1977): 73 - 86.

24. *Guy Livingstone: or "Thorough"* (London, 1857), p. 58.

25. See Malcom Elwin, *Victorian Wallflowers* (London, 1934), pp. 283ff.

26. "A Piece of Chalk," *Tremendous Trifles* (London, 1909), p. 3.

27. *Christowell: A Dartmoor Tale* (1881; rpt. London, 1893), p. 410.

28. Contemporary reviewers realized that Blackmore wrote with ancient myths in mind. His first two novels openly allude to the stories of Electra and of Adrastus; *Alice Lorraine* makes specific reference to Alcestis. But after all the Greek and Latin in *Cradock Nowell,* Blackmore allows only the epigraph from Theocritus, the allusions to Hercules, and a reference to Diana and Endymion as a parallel to Lorna and John; and he restricts John's Greek to little more than the verbs for striking and wounding and for loving (ch. 1)—the crucial actions of his initiation.

29. Margaret Oliphant, "Lorna Doone," *Blackwood's Magazine,* CIX (1871): 44.

30. See Burris, *Richard Doddridge Blackmore*, p. 70.

31. See Kerényi, p. 33.

32. *r.:. and Kitty: A Story of West Middlesex* (London, 1890), p. 357. This view of the hero's kinship with the villain was developed by Janet Pomeroy Blecha in her honors essay, "Approaches to *Lorna Doone*," University of Kansas, 1969. I am indebted to her study.

33. See Burris, p. 194.

34. See *Monographie de la Voie Sacrée Eleusinienne* (Paris, 1864), pp. 531 ff.

35. See Erich Neumann, *The Origins and History of Consciousness*, trans. R. F. Hull, I (New York, 1962), pp. 198, 216.

36. Frye, p. 195. Cf. the line beginning "Then is the faire White Woman / Married to the Ruddy Man," in Thomas Norton's *Ordinall of Alchemy*, Facsimile edition with introduction by E. J. Holmyard (London, 1927), p. 90.

37. Cicero, cited in note 7.

38. Budd, *The Last Victorian*, p. 62.

39. Cf. the comments by Blackmore's close friend Mortimer Collins: "The marriage of completion completes not only the characters and destinies of the two persons concerned, but likewise all their conceiveable functions. Comedies and novels are laughed at for ending with marriage, but the artist's unconscious instinct is true. To marry aright is to read the riddle of the world": *Mortimer Collins: his letters & friendships, with some account of his life*, ed. Frances Collins, II (London, 1877), p. 214.

40. "The Eleusinian Mysteries," *Contemporary Review*, XXXVIII (1880): 433. Much of this chapter appeared in *Nineteenth-century Fiction*, vol. 28, No. 4, pp. 435 - 449, ©1974 by The Regents of the University of California, and is reprinted by permission of The Regents.

Chapter Four

1. *The Maid of Sker* (1872; rpt. London, n.d.), p. 471; subsequent page references appear in the text.

2. No. 2164 (17 April 1869): 534 - 35.

3. To John Blackwood, misdated 31 January 1870. The apparent date is 31 January 1871, since Blackmore has just read a January 1871 review of *Lorna Doone*, or the date is 31 December 1870, if the review reached him early. Dates for other letters to John and William Blackwood in the National Library of Scotland will be given when possible in the text.

4. Mrs. Gerald Porter, ed., *William Blackwood and His Sons*, III (Edinburgh, 1898), p. 359.

5. See the letter to Macmillan in Buckler, p. 177.

6. 20 March 1873, UV.

7. See the informative essay by Sally Jones, "A Lost Leader: R. D. Blackmore and 'The Maid of Sker,'" *Anglo-Welsh Review*, XXV (Autumn 1975): 43.

8. The quotation is from Blackmore's letter to John Blackwood, 3 June 1872; Blackwood's letter about Froude and the bishop is dated only 21 December, but the year must be 1871.

9. Blackmore to Francis Armstrong, 2 August 1881, Dunn, p. 119.

10. To John Blackwood, 6 February 1872, NLS.

11. *Spectator* XLV (28 September 1872): 1241.

12. Jones, p. 43.

13. [John Hepburn Miller], "The Novels of Mr. Blackmore," *Blackwood's Magazine*, CLX (September 1896): 418.

14. See Jones, p. 40.

15. *Maxims*, II. 601 - 602, in *The Works of Hesiod, Callimachus, and Theognis*, trans. J. Banks (London, 1889), p. 251.

16. To Blackmore, 23 February and 5 October 1871, *William Blackwood and Sons*, III, 359 - 60.

17. No. 3,375 (5 October 1872): 987.

18. See Jones, p. 44.

19. To Blackmore, 4 October 1872, Dunn, p. 170.

20. See *Alice Lorraine: A Tale of the South Downs* (1875; rpt. London, n.d.), p. 1; subsequent page references appear in the text.

21. To John Blackwood, 23 February 1874, NLS.

22. Ibid.

23. Without knowing of the intended tragedy, Kenneth Budd applied this passage to the author's own predicament, p. 75.

24. To Mrs. Alfred William Hunt, 20 January 1875, Dunn, p. 119.

25. To George Eliot, 22 March 1860, *The George Eliot Letters*, ed. Gordon S. Haight, III (New Haven, 1954), p. 277.

26. K. Kerényi, *Eleusis: Archetypal Image of Mother and Daughter*, p. 55.

27. No. 2,479 (1 May 1875): 583.

28. XXXIX (15 May 1875): 633.

29. Stevenson's letter of thanks to Blackmore, 11 May 1889, is in the National Library of Scotland.

30. *Spectator*, XLVIII (10 July 1875): 885.

31. See Budd, p. 77, and Elwin, p. 269.

32. 7 May 1875, UV.

33. See Dunn, p. 230.

34. According to Blackmore's own "Notes" in "The Blackmore Family" file in the Westcountry Studies Library, he began *Cripps, the Carrier* on 13 August 1872; but he laid it aside to resume work on it on 18 May 1875.

35. Blackmore records these meetings and the letter in his "Notes" for 1875.

36. To Mrs. William Halliday, quoted with no date in "Blackmore's Letters," *Western Morning News*, 22 June 1925, Blackmore file, WSL.

37. Ll. 64 - 66, *The Complete Greek Drama*, ed. Whitney J. Oates and Eugene O'Neill, Jr., II (New York, 1938), p. 61.

38. XLIX (2 September 1876): 1103.

39. *Cripps, the Carrier: A Woodland Tale* (1876; rpt. London, n.d.) pp. 399 - 400; subsequent page references appear in the text.

40. Budd, p. 79.

41. *Spectator,* op. cit.

42. 9 March 1876, UV.

43. 7 February 1876, UV. Quoted by permission of Professor Quentin Bell.

44. *The Women of Trachis,* 11. 529 - 30, trans. Michael Jameson, *The Complete Greek Tragedies,* ed. David Greene and Richmond Lattimore, II (Chicago, 1959), p. 297.

45. George Burnett Smith, "Mr. Blackmore's Novels," *International Review,* VII (October 1877): 409.

46. Budd, p. 82.

47. *Spectator,* L (24 November 1877): 1476.

48. *Saturday Review,* XLII (8 July 1876): 54.

49. To William Blackwood, 16 January 1872, NLS.

50. 7 May 1875, UV. Hardy's letter to Blackmore of 8 June 1875 says that he had not read *Lorna Doone* before writing *Far From the Madding Crowd.*

51. See Dunn, p. 164.

52. To William Blackwood, 21 November 1876, NLS.

53. To J. M. Winn, 19 February 1890, UV.

54. To Showell Rogers, 30 December 1895, UV.

Chapter Five

1. *Perlycross: A Tale of the Western Hills* (London, 1894), pp. 128 - 29.

2. Dunn, p. 114.

3. Bk. III, 11. 69 - 73, trans. Robert Fitzgerald (Garden City, 1963), p. 37.

4. *Mary Anerley: A Yorkshire Tale* (London, 1880), p. 72; subsequent page references appear in the text.

5. Quoted in William C. Frierson, *The English Novel in Transition, 1885 - 1940* (Norman, Oklahoma, 1942), p. 5.

6. See the enthusiastic reviews in the *Athenaeum,* No. 2,742 (15 May 1880): 630, and the *Saturday Review,* XLIX (29 May 1880): 701.

7. *Spectator,* LIII (7 August 1880): 1010.

8. To Edward Marston, 5 November 1888, UV.

9. *The Remarkable History of Sir Thomas Upmore, Bart., M.P.,* I (London, 1884), p. 49; subsequent page references appear in the text.

10. Blackmore's translation of his Latin verses on the removal of Blundell's School in *Exeter and Plymouth Gazette,* 11 June 1882, WSL.

11. 6 February 1883, UV.

12. See Owen's anonymous review, "Darwin on the Origin of Species," *Edinburgh Review,* CXI (1860): 256ff.; and Chapter XV of *The Origin of*

Species, 6th edition, 1872, in *Darwin*, ed. Philip Appleman (New York, 1970), p. 185.

13. 20 December 1883, UV.
14. *Christowell: A Dartmoor Tale* (1881; rpt. London, 1893), p. 304; subsequent page references appear in the text. The epigraph, *Splendidè mendax*, is from Bk. III, Ode 22 of Horace, and it refers to the captain's lying in order to bear the blame for his older brother's cowardice.
15. *The Poems of William Barnes*, ed. Bernard Jones, I (London, 1962), p. 245.
16. See *The Labouring Life* (London, 1932), p. 17.
17. *The Two Widecombe Tracts, 1638, Giving a Contemporary Account of the Great Storm, reprinted with an Introduction* (Exeter, 1905), p. 4.
18. John Prince, *Worthies of Devon* (1701; rpt. Plymouth, 1810), p. 570.
19. From "A Short Description of the Parish. . . ," attributed to the Rev. George Lyde, who was in the pulpit when the storm hit, printed in *Things New and Old Concerning the Parish of Widecombe-in-the-Moor and its Neighbourhood*, ed. Robert Dymond (Torquay, 1876), p. 108.
20. *The Two Widecombe Tracts*, p. 8. Blackmore could have read this account in the inclusive second tract, reprinted by Dymond in 1876 in *Things New and Old*. . . .
21. Budd identifies "Springhaven" with Newhaven, p. 97.
22. *Athenaeum*, No. 3,099 (19 March 1887): 375.
23. *Springhaven: A Tale of the Great War*, intro. R. L. Blackmore (London 1969), p. 327; subsequent page references appear in the text.
24. Elwin, p. 281.
25. This point comes from R. L. Blackmore's introduction to the novel.
26. *Spectator*, LX (19 March 1887): 392.
27. To Coventry Patmore, 7 May 1888, *Further Letters of Gerard Manley Hopkins*, ed. Claude Colleer Abbott (London, 1938), p. 241.
28. Ibid.

Chapter Six

1. Blackmore to Edwin Jacobs, 6 November 1894, quoted by permission of the Vicar and Parish of Culmstock.
2. Quoted in Dunn, p. 251.
3. Hall Caine, "The New Watchwords of Fiction," *Contemporary Review*, LVII (1890): 480, 485.
4. *Kit and Kitty: A Story of West Middlesex* (1889; rpt. New York, 1890), p. 4; subsequent page references appear in the text.
5. See the *Spectator*, LXIV (23 January 1890): 123.
6. Caine, "The New Watchwords of Fiction," p. 480.
7. *Perlycross: A Tale of the Western Hills* (London, 1894), p. 416; subsequent page references appear in the text.
8. Robert Lawson, 13 May 1890, UV.

9. Quoted in Dunn, p. 239.

10. 2 November 1894, UV.

11. Quoted in Dunn, pp. 239 - 240.

12. Caine, *My Story*, p. 302.

13. William Doble, "Culmstock," *Devonia*, I (1904): 297. For details about the setting, see A. B. Blackmore "R. D. Blackmore and Culmstock," *Devon Life*, VI (May 1970): 14 - 15.

14. "Old Times at Culmstock," *Tiverton Gazette*, 4 August 1925, Culmstock File at WSL. The cholera is mentioned on p. 111 of *Perlycross*.

15. F. J. Snell, *The Blackmore Country* (1906; rev. ed. London, 1911), p. 20.

16. Ibid., p. 17.

17. "A Village Story. Culmstock" (1956), WSL. This pamphlet was prepared by Mrs. M. J. Saunders, using notes by Mr. R. A. Bull.

18. "A Culmstock Oak with a History," *Tiverton Gazette*, 28 March 1931, WSL.

19. "Old Times at Culmstock," *Tiverton Gazette*, 25 July 1925, WSL; this source lists 143 people on regular out-door relief in 1833 in the parish, many of these being heads of families. When the plans to build a workhouse were announced in 1835, the overseers claimed that there were 269 paupers in the parish; the workhouse was to hold no more than 100 of them (4 August 1925).

20. "Old Times at Culmstock," *Tiverton Gazette*, 4 August 1925, WSL.

21. See F. J. Snell, *Early Associations of Archbishop Temple: A Record of Blundell's School and Its Neighbourhood* (London, 1904), pp. 74 - 75. Snell misleadingly gives the impression that Temple was still at Culmstock in 1835.

22. For a discussion of the "ceremonial regime," see the opening section of E. W. Martin's book *The Shearers and the Shorn: A Study of Life in a Devon Community* (London, 1965).

23. Budd, p. 110.

24. John Barrell and John Bull, eds., *A Book of English Pastoral Verse* (London, 1975), p. 4.

25. See W. J. Keith, *The Rural Tradition: William Cobbett, Gilbert White, and Other Non-Fiction Prose Writers of the English Countryside* (North Brighton, 1975), p. 98.

26. *Academy* XLVII (20 October 1894): 299.

27. [John Hepburn Miller], "The Novels of Mr. Blackmore," *Blackwood's Magazine*, CLX (September 1896): 413.

28. See *Saturday Review*, LXVIII (29 September 1894): 360.

29. No. 3,488 (1 September 1894): 285.

30. William Doble, "Richard Doddridge Blackmore," *Devonia*, IV (1906): 33.

31. See Mircea Eliade, *The Sacred and the Profane*, trans. Willard Trask (New York, 1959), pp. 22ff.

32. See Snell, *The Blackmore Country*, pp. 38, 41.

33. According to Peter Haining in *The Legend and Bizarre Crimes of Spring Heeled Jack* (London, 1977), no reports of this figure appeared before 1837, two years after the action begins in *Perlycross*. Haining identifies him with the young and eccentric Lord Waterford.

34. John Blackmore's role in restoring Culmstock Church was less important than it sounds in the novel, since the major expansion was done in 1825, ten years before his arrival. The rood screen had been found before he came, but the removal of the gallery (called "hideous" in the novel) and the placement of the screen under the east window apparently were accomplished during his curacy (1835 - 41). A report in 1845 says that the reredos formed of the stone screen "was restored a few years since" and notes the addition of a clerestory "about five years since": "Report of Visiting Committee, Read at a quarterly meeting of the Exeter Diocesan Architectural Society . . . Nov. 13, 1845," *Transactions of the Exeter Diocesan Society*, II (1847): 129 - 30. However, John Blackmore did play a major role in rebuilding the church at Asford, North Devon, in 1854, and he helped to pay for the project.

35. *Cradock Nowell*, p. 416.

Chapter Seven

1. To J. M. Winn, 4 March 1884, UV.

2. "Richard Doddridge Blackmore: A Note," *Critic*, LXXXVII (1901): 413.

3. From the notebook bound with a cover of *Perlycross*, UE (University of Exeter).

4. See his letter to F. B. Doveton, 9 December 1894, UV.

5. To Mrs. Mortimer Collins, 12 February 1877, UE.

6. Two fragments of the opening scene are in the University of Exeter Library.

7. 19 June 1895, NLS.

8. William Blackwood to Blackmore, 21 June 1895, NLS.

9. To Charles Ballard, 13 November 1895, Dunn,p. 246; to Mackenzie Bell, 13 December 1895, UV.

10. 2 September 1896, NLS.

11. 9 October 1896, NLS.

12. 2 December 1895, NLS.

13. 9 October 1896, NLS.

14. *Dariel: A Romance of Surrey* (Edinburgh, 1897), p. 453; subsequent page references are given in the text.

15. 29 December 1896, NLS.

16. See R. L. Blackmore's development of this point in the Everyman edition of *Lorna Doone* (London, 1966), pp. vii - viii.

17. To William Blackwood, 2 December 1896, NLS.

18. Ibid.

19. To William Blackwood, 22 December 1896, NLS.

20. To Charles Ballard, 9 August 1896, Dunn, p. 247.

21. To R. W. Sawtell, 20 August 1897, Dunn, p. 248.

22. No. 3,658 (4 December 1897): 682.

Chapter Eight

1. To Mackenzie Bell, 21 June 1894, UV.

2. *Athenaeum*, No. 3,658 (4 December, 1897), p. 782.

3. Quoted by W. W. Joyce, "[Blackmore:] Tribute to His Life and Work," *Western Morning News* (Exeter), in "Blackmore Family" Notes, WSL.

4. To J. M. Winn, 4 March 1884, UV.

5. *Christowell*, p. 252. On "interthought," see James Baker, *Literary and Biographical Studies* (London, 1908), p. 34.

6. See Burris, pp. 167 - 68.

7. To Mortimer Collins, 20 March 1873, UV.

8. Florence Hardy, *The Early Life of Thomas Hardy, 1840 - 1891* (London, 1928), p. 231.

9. See Northrop Frye, *A Natural Perspective: The Development of Shakespearean Comedy and Romance* (New York, 1965), p. 4.

10. *Athenaeum*, No. 3,099 (19 March 1887): 375.

11. *Spectator*, XLIX (2 September 1876): 1103.

12. [Anon.], "The Sincerest Form of Flattery. III. Of Mr. R. D. Blackmore," *Cornhill Magazine*, LXII (1890): 374.

13. Rider Haggard, "About Fiction," *Contemporary Review*, LI (1887): 175.

14. George Burnett Smith, "Mr. Blackmore's Novels," *International Review*, VII (1877): 408.

15. See Burris, pp. 161ff.

16. "Richard Doddridge Blackmore: A Note," *Critic*, LXXXVII (1901): 414.

17. "Christowell," *Journal of Forestry and Estate Management*, VII (1883): 726.

18. "General Preface to the Wessex Edition of 1912," rpt. in *Tess of the d'Urbervilles*, ed. P. N. Furbank (London, 1974), p. 475.

19. Eden Phillpotts, *From the Angle of 88* (London, 1951), p. 69.

20. *Tess of the d'Urbervilles*, p. 168.

21. Phillpotts, "Richard Doddridge Blackmore: a Note," p. 414.

22. *From the Angle of 88*, p. 17.

23. "Richard Doddridge Blackmore: a Note," p. 414.

24. "General Preface to the Wessex Edition of 1912," in *Tess*, p. 477.

25. *Christowell*, p. 301.

Selected Bibliography

PRIMARY SOURCES

Among Blackmore's manuscripts at the University of Exeter are several poems, parts of plays, and two stories, "Our Barge" and "Tiarka," all of which apparently were never published.

1. Books

Poems by Melanter. London: Robert Hardwicke, 1854.

Epullia. London: Hope and Company, 1854.

The Bugle of the Black Sea. London: Robert Hardwicke, 1855.

The Fate of Franklin. London: Robert Hardwicke, 1860.

The Farm and Fruit of Old. London: Low, 1862.

Clara Vaughan: A Novel. London: Macmillan, 1864. Serialized in *Cassell's Illustrated Family Paper* as *The Purpose of a Life,* 12 March 1864 - 6 August 1864.

Cradock Nowell: A Tale of the New Forest. London: Chapman and Hall, 1866. Serialized in *Macmillan's Magazine,* May 1865 - August 1866.

Lorna Doone: A Romance of Exmoor. London: Low, 1869.

The Georgics of Virgil. London: Low, 1871.

The Maid of Sker. Edinburgh and London: Blackwood, 1872. Serialized in *Blackwood's Magazine,* August 1871 - July 1872.

Alice Lorraine: A Tale of the South Downs. London: Low, 1875. Serialized in *Blackwood's Magazine,* March 1874 - April 1875, except November 1874.

Cripps, the Carrier: A Woodland Tale. London: Low, 1876. Serialized in the *Graphic,* 1 January 1876 - 10 June 1876, and in *Harper's Weekly Magazine,* 15 January 1876 - 24 June 1876.

Erēma: Or My Father's Sin. London: Smith, Elder, 1877. Serialized in the *Cornhill Magazine,* November 1876 - November 1877.

Mary Anerley: A Yorkshire Tale. London: Low, 1880. Serialized in *Fraser's Magazine,* July 1879 - September 1880; and in *Harper's Monthly Magazine,* August 1879 - August 1880.

Christowell: A Dartmoor Tale. London: Low, 1881. Serialized in *Good Words,* January - December 1881.

The Remarkable History of Sir Thomas Upmore, Bart, M. P., formerly known as "Tommy Upmore." London: Low, 1884.

Springhaven: A Tale of the Great War. London: Low, 1887. Serialized in

Harper's Monthly Magazine, April 1886 - April 1887, except December 1886.

Kit and Kitty: A Story of West Middlesex. London: Low, 1889. Serialized in the *Queen*, 6 July 1889 - 22 March 1890.

Perlycross: A Tale of the Western Hills. London: Low, 1894. Serialized in *Macmillan's Magazine*, June 1893 - July 1894.

Fringilla, or Tales in Verse. London: Elkin Matthews, 1895.

Tales from the Telling House. London: Low, 1896. Published without Blackmore's Preface as *Slain by the Doones*. New York: Dodd, Mead, 1895.

Dariel: A Romance of Surrey. Edinburgh and London: Blackwood, 1897. Serialized in *Blackwood's Magazine*, October 1896 - October 1897.

2. Uncollected Poems, Essays, and Stories

"Books for Review . . . Poems by A. J. Mumby" *(sic)*. *Woolman's Exeter and Plymouth Gazette*, LXIV (3 July 1852): 6.

"Sicilian Hours." *Dublin University Magazine*, XLVI (August 1855): 201 - 207.

"Trite Songs Turned Anew by a Novelist." *Gentleman's Magazine*, XII N.S. (January - April 1874): "The Sparrow" (Catullus: *Carm*. ii), 44; "The Sparrow's Death" (Catullus: *Carm*. iii), 168; "Lydia" (Horace: *Carm*. iii. 9), 300. "The Sneezes" (Catullus: *Carm*. xlv), 452.

"A Statesman of an Old School" (Horace: *Odes* iii 5). *University Magazine* N.S. I (January 1878): 47 - 48.

"Dominus Illuminatio Mea." *University Magazine*, III N.S. (February 1879): 187.

"Effosus Queritur Petrus" and "Solatur Alumnus" (verses on the removal of Blundell's School). *Exeter and Plymouth Gazette*, CIX (17 June 1881): 8.

"Not Until Next Time." *Blackwood's Magazine*, CXXXV (January 1884): 64.

"Mr. Giffen and John Bull," *National Review*, IV (January 1885): 658 - 59.

"Dimidium Facti." *Harper's Monthly Magazine*, LXXI (October 1885): 683.

"The Enemies of the Vine." *Journal of the Royal Horticultural Society*, XIII (September 1891): 45 - 56.

"A Part: Greater than the Whole." *Atalanta*, Christmas Number, 1895.

"Leila; or, the Golden Fleece" (short story). *Boston Evening Transcript* 1, 4, 5, 6 January 1897.

"Carmen Britanicum." *Publisher's Circular*, LXVI (12 June 1897): 707.

"The Brook by the Thames" (short story). *St James Budget*, Christmas Number, 1898.

SECONDARY SOURCES

BAKER, JAMES. *Literary and Biographical Studies*. London: Chapman and

Hall, 1908. Chapter on Blackmore gives a clear portrait of him in old age, with preceptive comments on his style.

BLACKMORE, A. B. "R. D. Blackmore and Culmstock." *Devon Life*, VI (May 1970): 14 - 15. Presents some hitherto unpublished facts about the novelist's family and describes the setting that inspired *Perlycross*.

BUCKLER, WILLIAM E. "Blackmore's Novels before 'Lorna Doone.'" *Nineteenth-Century Fiction*, X (December 1955): 169 - 87. Presents the letters to Macmillan.

BUDD, KENNETH. *The Last Victorian: R. D. Blackmore and His Novels*. London: Centaur Press, 1960. Brief critical survey with sound evaluations and comments on Blackmore's relation to other novelists of his era.

———; Nikolai Tolstoy, John Yeowell, et al. *Blackmore Studies*, I (Redhill, Surrey: Surrey Fine Art Press, 1969) Published for the centenary of *Lorna Doone*; contains factual notes and lively appreciations.

BURRIS, QUINCY GUY. *Richard Doddridge Blackmore: His Life and Novels*. Urbana: University of Illinois Studies in Language and Literature, 1930. The pioneer study, outdated now in biographical matters but still useful in relating Blackmore to other writers.

BURTON, S. H. *The Lorna Doone Trail*. Williton, Somerset: Exmoor Press, 1975. A short photographic essay on the Doone Country with brief comments by an expert on the topography and traditions of Exmoor.

DUNN, W. H. *R. D. Blackmore: the Author of "Lorna Doone."* London: Robert Hale, 1956. The only biography, worshipful in tone, inaccurate on the career of the novelist's father, but the most informative book yet on Blackmore; especially useful in showing his wide circle of correspondents. Lengthy bibliography.

ELLIS, STEWART MARSH. *Wilkie Collins, Le Fanu, and Others*. London: Constable, 1931. Lively biographical and critical chapter on Blackmore.

ELWIN, MALCOLM. *Victorian Wallflowers*. London: Jonathan Cape, 1934. Chapter on Blackmore relates his fiction to the tastes of late-Victorian readers and to comparable novels of the time.

JONES, SALLY. "A Lost Leader: R. D. Blackmore and 'The Maid of Sker,'" *Anglo-Welsh Review*, XXV (Autumn 1975): 32 - 45. Presents Blackmore's Welsh heritage and interprets the novel from a Welsh point of view.

LARTER, C. ETHELINDA. "R. D. Blackmore and 'Christowell,'" *Transactions of the Devonshire Association for the Advancement of Science, Literature and Art*, L (1918): 382 - 90. Presents information about the setting of this novel.

[MILLAR, JOHN HEPBURN]. "The Novels of Mr. Blackmore." *Blackwood's Magazine*, CLX (September 1896): 409 - 22. A generally admiring survey at the close of his career.

PHILLPOTTS, EDEN. "Richard Doddridge Blackmore: A Note." *Critic*,

XXXVIII (May 1900): 413 - 15. One of several eulogistic comments by his successor in Devon fiction.

SMITH, GEORGE BURNETT. "Mr. Blackmore's Novels." *International Review,* VII (October 1879): 406 - 26. An early attempt to defend Blackmore's romantic vision of human character.

SNELL, F. J. *The Blackmore Country.* Second Edition (revised). London: Adam and Charles Black, 1911. Despite some inaccuracies, this remains the best book-length exploration of the Devon settings of *Perlycross, Lorna Doone,* and *The Maid of Sker.*

SUTTON, MAX KEITH. "Blackmore's Letters to Blackwood: the Record of a Novelist's Indecision." *English Literature in Transition: 1880 - 1920,* XX (1977): 69 - 76. Shows his difficulties in writing *The Maid of Sker* and *Alice Lorraine.*

THORNICROFT, L. B. *The Story of the Doones in Fact, Fiction and Photo.* Third Edition (enlarged). Taunton: Wessex Press, 1947. One of numerous attempts to establish the relations among history, legend, and fiction, this guide to the region accepts the belief that the Doones really lived upon Exmoor.

Index